11/99

BIG CITY LOOK

BIG CITY LOOK

NEW YORK CITY
LOS ANGELES
CHICAGO
WASHINGTON, D.C.
DALLAS
ATLANTA
HOW TO
ACHIEVE
THAT
METROPOLITAN
CHIC—
NO MATTER
WHERE
YOU
LIVE

VINCENT ROPPATTE
AND SHERRY SUIB COHEN

Photographs by Alex Cao   Illustrations by Akiko Oguro

Cliff Street Books

An Imprint of HarperCollinsPublishers

HarperCollins books may be purchased for educational, business, or sales promotional use. For information please write: Special Markets Department, HarperCollins Publishers, Inc., 10 East 53rd Street, New York, NY 10022.

FIRST EDITION

Designed by Robbin Gourley

ISBN 0-06-017589-3

98 99 00 01 02 ❖/RRD 10 9 8 7 6 5 4 3 2 1

For my wife, Frances, and my children, Dawn and Jude.
Family is all.

Dedicated to Connie Clausen.
She had The Look, she had the style, she had the wit, she had the great heart.
She *lived*.

CONTENTS

CHAPTER THREE: FACE

CHAPTER FOUR: ATTITUDE

EPILOGUE

ACKNOWLEDGMENTS

FOREWORD
DIANE SAWYER

You know how it is. Some days the mirror is a doorway to despair. Your skin is in armed rebellion. Your hair looks like something you forgot to take off last Halloween. Your clothes seem like a joke your closet cooked up overnight. So what are you going to do?

You could phone the plastic surgeons with the drive-through service. Or hire David Copperfield and his army of illusionists.

Or, my recommendation, spend one hour alone with Vincent.

I wish you could be there with us Wednesday nights at the ABC studio before our live television news magazine goes on the air. I show up from some investigation or war zone. He's just spent a breathlessly long day transforming the fashionable and famous people of New York. In he sails with some new and exotic coffee to drink, tea bags for my eyes, and the latest

Diane Sawyer, a spectacular woman and friend, in Adrienne Vittadini's black cashmere sweater and Ted Muehling's gold earrings. Vincent wears his customary black.

dream potion for my frequent-flyer skin.

He tells funny stories. He gentles me into confidence.

Then, of course, he redoes my clothes. One time he took off his shirt and made me wear it. Another time I wore his belt. At my interview with the Clintons, I was wearing Vincent's coat.

As for hair, Vincent is justifiably a legend, with amazing talent for all those cutting/drying/sparkling/arranging things. But he knows the tender secret: that hair is simply high school, riding around on your head. When it's right, you're the queen of the prom. When it's not, no one will ever ask you out anywhere again. He has a brilliant instinct for that place where inner feelings and outer appearance meet.

I think that's because his gifts are equaled only by his heart. Anyone at ABC can ask Vincent for help (and most do), and he'll give them the same gift of time and insight and artistry he gives all those movie and society stars. He is simply one of the most generous and loving people on the face of the earth.

So enjoy this book as you would a visit with a kindhearted magician. A world-class stylist. A down-home friend. He has spent his life in demand by the rich and flashy and famous. But I know Vincent, and if he could go door to door every day and help every one of us face the mirror with joy, that's what he would really want to do.

From my collection of precious grooming tools that the legends gave me as gifts. In her will, Marlene Dietrich bequeathed to me her favorite handkerchief, the glass (with a real ruby) in which she kept her makeup brushes, and the two mirrors she always carried with her when she toured—one a regular hand mirror and the other a portable mirror. It was her firm ritual to take a quick look in one of these mirrors just before she went onstage to convince herself that she really was Marlene Dietrich. The mirror case has her fingerprint in lipstick—her "inscription" to me. Kate Hepburn used to roll her fine hair with handmade rollers she'd created herself from the *New York Times*—this roller is inscribed to me. And the brush is Melina Mercouri's—I treasure the blond hair still caught in its bristles.

PREFACE
MY VINCENT: A SHORT BIO
Sherry Suib Cohen

Walk into the Saks Fifth Avenue beauty salon on New York's Fifth Avenue. It's an experience. Perhaps you'll see one or more Miss Americas (Vincent was a long-time consultant to the Miss America Pageant) sitting next to writer Betty Friedan, who's sitting near gossip queen Liz

Smith, who's chatting with an exquisite Ford model, who's sitting next to a legal secretary, who's next to the youngest woman president of a huge corporation, who's next to Liza Minnelli, who's whispering to Broadway star Elaine Stritch, who's sitting next to somebody's mom, who's trying not to stare at Ethel Kennedy. They're all waiting patiently for Vincent. And then Vincent magically transforms us all. My Vincent. We all call him that—my Vincent. Society grandes dames, movie stars, businesswomen, lowly journalists. We're all very proprietorial about the man.

The first and second times I sat in Vincent's chair I firmly told him:

Eighteen—and excited about my future. Little did I know how exciting it would be.

No artificial color for me! He cut my graying hair and made me look—well, prettier. The third time he gently fingered my hair, sighed, and asked me to trust him. I said I would—and he quickly applied the color I'd sworn I'd never allow. Forget natural. My heart was in my mouth.

An hour later I was a living doll. Even Vincent couldn't help swooning at his own alchemy. As the years passed, he gentled and made gorgeous my nervous daughter and future daughter-in-law for their weddings, worried about me, called the head of the orthopedic department when I had a medical problem (Vincent knows *everyone*), yelled at me when I wasn't positive enough for his eternally optimistic nature, and never failed to make me look like a living doll.

And he does the same for everyone, this man with the golden hands.

He began a meteoric rise in the world of style and fashion at seventeen, when he won the World International Styling Competition in New York in the early sixties, and was invited by Enrico Caruso to work in his East Side salon. On day one he told Vincent, "Go do Ginger

Rogers—she's in booth two." Vincent didn't miss a beat, and within months the precocious youngster was styling Audrey Hepburn, Melina Mercouri, Grace Kelly, and Joan Crawford for starring roles. Soon he joined the on-the-road shows of Marlene Dietrich and Judy Garland. After eighteen years he left Caruso to head Bergdorf Goodman's beauty salon, and in the early nineties Vincent was asked to become Saks Fifth Avenue's master stylist.

What everyone knows is that he's a workaholic—often opening Saks at six A.M. for working clients who have no other free time. It's also well known that he's a serious jock, he jogs, he plays intense tennis, and every week another beautiful person asks him to be her escort as she gets an award, opens in a Broadway show, or chairs a prestigious charity event. What few know is that his strength comes from a deeply religious nature (he won't tell you, for example, but I will, that all his proceeds from this book are going to St. Jude Children's Research Hospital in Memphis, Tennessee). Few also know of his intense family feeling and the love he derives from Frances, whom he married when they were both teenagers, and from his children, who call him daily.

I've never met a person with a better eye for style. Until I saw it, I'd never have believed that a man with such immense talent would give the same loving care and time to the thinning-hair problems of a cancer survivor he's just met as he gives to the president's wife. I've never met a professional more beloved by his clients.

My Vincent.

INTRODUCTION
WHO IS THE WOMAN WITH THE BIG CITY LOOK?

One brisk fall morning you find yourself alone in a big city somewhere in America. Strolling down its most famous avenue, you're feeling great as you take in the luxurious department stores and the stately churches. But wait! Suddenly, your attention is captured by one single woman in the horde of passersby. She's marvelous!

You know staring is rude, but the woman swinging by radiates such style, such energy, such ease—you can't take your eyes off her. Trying to be discreet, you slowly turn to watch her

From left to right, top to bottom: Cynthia McFadden; Julia Ormond; Phyllis George; Kathie Lee Gifford; Isabella Rossellini; Liz Smith; Adrienne Vittadini and her husband, Gigi; Rose Marie Bravo; and Natalie Cole.

progress down the avenue. You're not the only one. Admiring glances are everywhere.

You've all noticed the woman with the Big City Look. Sure you have. She's a stunner. She's probably not a perfect beauty, nor does she wear the most expensive or trendy clothes, but there is just something about her that's extraordinary: it's confidence, it's an unwavering *put-together* look. Her hair is swingy and shiny, her makeup is simple but luscious, her clothes are classic. Then there's her walk: She's confidence personified in the way she holds her shoulders, her head.

The Look does not read small-town cute. It is cosmopolitan. It says grace and elegance. It says charisma. And something inside you says... *I wish I looked like that.*

You can. The Big City Look doesn't require a flawless face or body. Good taste and high style are necessary, but you can develop those things. And here's more good news: The Big City Look is not found only in big cities. Some women who live in small-town America have learned it or instinctively have it—that indefinable, marvelous chic that opens doors, tells people before you even open your mouth that you're not only stunning, you're knowing, intelligent, daring.

Here's the bottom line: If you can pick out The Look, if you have ever recognized it on another woman, you instinctively know what it's all about. You may not have been born with the ability to put yourself together with terrific style—but I'm here to tell you, if you can spot it, you can plot it. You can acquire that metropolitan polish. It's waiting for you in these pages.

SO WHO IS SHE?

Oh, she's been around for decades, for centuries. Cleopatra had The Look in 44 B.C., and Marie Antoinette had it in 1785. Isabella Rossellini and Vanessa Williams have it today. So does Diane Sawyer. So does Winona Ryder. Maybe your neighbor has it.

The first time I saw a woman with The Look, I was seventeen years old. She came into Enrico Caruso's beauty salon, where I was serving an apprenticeship—and my jaw just dropped. I was very new at the beauty business, but even then I knew it when I saw it—that stunning, sure, cosmopolitan style. Her name was Audrey Hepburn. Although I couldn't wait to get my hands on her hair, when she sat in my chair, my hands shook. Oh yes—she had that look.

As the months of my apprenticeship passed, the most marvelous women in the world sat in my chair—directed there by Caruso, the master in the business. The women with the Big City Look in those days carried legendary names—Ginger Rogers, Suzy Parker, Jennifer Jones, Marlene Dietrich, Judy Garland. They were my earliest icons of a certain kind of style—*not* girl-next-door-ish, *not* vampish, *not* even simply pretty. No, their style was born of a sophisticated beauty. I watched them carefully; I wanted to learn their innate sense of quality. Their sureness of what was right for them was intoxicating. Dietrich strode into the salon in the mannish pants no other woman then dreamed of wearing. Jennifer Jones sported the romantic, smooth Marienbad pageboy later to be immortalized in countless other films. The glamour of the stars was undeniable, but I also spotted The Look on others—on hardworking women with limited budgets. And I learned something vital: The Look had nothing to do with wealth or age; it was priceless and ageless.

I noticed that The Look seemed to change from city to city: There always was and always will be a conspicuous absence of sterling silver conch belts and pretty prairie skirts in Manhattan, but women with The Look can't live without them in Dallas. Though it changes regionally, The Look is recognizable anywhere.

What's *not* The Look is also instantly recognizable. Recently, we were photographing the extraordinary journalist Cynthia McFadden for this book. Cynthia, the spiritual goddaughter of Katharine Hepburn, the woman who may have *invented* the Big City Look, told me a wonderful story that seems to say it all.

"Katharine and I were riding along through the streets of New York in the back of her car," Cynthia remembers with a chuckle, "passing one shlumpy young woman after another. One with great, fat, sloppy khaki pants; another with an oversize, ripped man's shirt. They were caricatures of the woman who sat beside me, who wore khakis and men's shirts with such style. And Katharine was just terribly upset, shaking her head in dismay.

"'What's the matter?' I asked her.

"'It's all my fault,' she groaned in those wonderful, quavery, clipped vowels. 'This is not what I had in mind, not what I had in mind at all.'"

WHAT GIVES HER THE BIG CITY LOOK?

Her Hair

One thing I clearly knew, even in those early years: The *Big City Look* always included great hair. If hair was long and loose, it was clean and shiny and swingy. That hair moved, that hair bounced. If the hair was short, it often had a slightly tousled flair, a healthy, lustrous quirkiness—maybe an asymmetrical part, maybe wild, wanton bangs. If the hair was pulled back, it was sleek and soigné, very worldly. If it was a blunt bob, you could cut your fingers on the line that sliced along the jawbone. The message? It was true in the Audrey Hepburn days, as it is today, that the woman with the Big City Look has definite hair—no wishy-washy curls that don't know where they want to fall. Even in the days when head-hugging, perfectly permed little waves were popular, the woman with the Big City Look (with the possible exception of Norma Shearer) opted for a more natural style.

Her Fashion Sense

I look at those legendary stars from my youth and compare them to this decade's icons: Brooke Astor, Nina Griscom, and the late Jackie Kennedy Onassis—women like that. Today's icons of great fashion, like yesteryear's, are not fashion victims. They wear clothes that are largely unembellished and classic in line, that do not slavishly reflect what's in the magazines that minute. Still, those clothes have high style, even in their simplicity. *Especially* in their simplicity.

Whatever her figure, if the woman with the Big City Look is wearing jeans, they fit and they're basic and they are simple—as jeans are supposed to be; very few women with The Look have jeweled studs on their jeans. Whatever her figure, the stunning woman's clothes are made from good fabrics. An understated purity makes them stand out. Whatever her figure, the woman with The Look takes chances—risks that make her look unique but are always in good taste and always appropriate. Whether it's an interesting color combination, an unexpected fabric mix, or a piece of vintage jewelry perched high on a shoulder, she's a standout.

Her Face

I can guarantee it—you won't find a slash of garish rouge on those cheek-bones. You will find a clean, delicately made up visage that radiates good health and beauty. The woman with The Look knows the subtle techniques of skin care and makeup. She wears colors that are flattering to her individual skin shade—and she's not one bit tempted by the silly and excessive makeup palettes of glaring colors with which merchandisers entice customers. When was the last time you saw aquamarine eyelids on a woman with The Look? You have *never* seen aquamarine eyelids on that woman. She's her own woman and it shows in her makeup, in the luminosity of her skin, in her smile.

Her Attitude

Perhaps this is where the woman with the Big City Look is most easily recognizable. She has that panache, the sophisticated quality that is so essential to a great cosmopolitan look. She's intimate with the beauty benefits of serenity. She's secure. She likes herself. She has inner resources: Although she's warm and friendly to others, she never minds being alone. She's a feminist and a babe at the same time. She's learned the inescapable truth that even if perfect features come from genes, attitude never does. That marvelous-looking woman had to work to develop those tools of attitude. Somewhere along the line—you'd better believe it—she found people and strategies to help her.

So who is the woman with the Big City Look?

With a little effort, and a lot of fun in the process of learning, she could be you.

CHAPTER ONE
HAIR

THE NAKED LADY

A long time ago, in the eleventh century, there lived a kind and beautiful woman who gave new meaning to hair. Her husband, Leofric, earl of Mercia, was a killjoy and imposed a terrible tax on his people. When the gentle lady begged Leofric to rescind the tax, he said he'd do it only if she would ride naked on a horse through town at noon. Well, being a doll, she did, directing her people not to look. One guy did look, was struck blind, and was forever after known as Peeping Tom. True story.

Who was the woman? Her name, of course, was Lady Godiva, and she wasn't really so brave because she knew her marvelous, hip-length golden hair (the Big City Look for eleventh-century Coventry) would cover her nakedness. Fabulous hair saved the day. It usually does.

The fabulous model Silke in a yellow-sashed blue Versace gown.

Hair's magic. It may not be so easy to take off the twenty pounds or the eye overhang, but you can walk into the salon of a great hairstylist and change your mood, maybe even your life—immediately. Generally, instant gratification doesn't come so easily.

START AT THE TOP

Diana Vreeland once said that a woman's style starts with her hair and moves downward to her clothes. She was right. The Big City Look starts at the top.

What if you started with your clothes? Disaster. Women with great style rarely go shopping on a bad-hair day. No outfit, no matter how spectacular or costly, will look good. On the other hand, if your hair looks wonderful, you wear even the most ordinary clothes with stylish ease. You stand taller, feel prettier, truly look prettier.

Going for a serious job interview? Visit your stylist before you shop for the interview outfit. He'll give you a seriously stunning presence—and then you can go out to find the fashion to match.

Need to look elegantly outrageous—just for today? Start at the top: A good stylist will make sure the outrageous hair is temporary and will last no longer than your mood. Then go buy the funky fashion.

Here's the best news: Hair is, without a doubt, the *easiest* place to start to get the Big City Look. Hair isn't permanent—like broad, Venusian hips. Even if your hair is overbleached, oversunned, overcolored, overcut, under cared for, you always have another chance when it grows back. Hips are a lot harder to fix. Also, fabulous hair has a way of diverting attention from problem hips, problem weight, problem anything. Hair is the best place to risk change. It's hair. It grows back. When you finally find a great new hairstyle that really works for you, positive changes in the way you dress will probably follow.

BE FUSSY WHEN CHOOSING A HAIRSTYLIST

The operative word on selecting a hairstylist is "expectation." *Expect* the best. Expect an artist stylist who looks at you hard, who doesn't start cutting mindlessly, but carefully checks you out, asks questions about your lifestyle, pays attention to the person—not just the hair—in the chair.

Expect the process to take time. My customers sometimes complain that it takes forever. That's true—for everyone, not just the rich and famous. I can have Jamie Lee Curtis or the girl next door in my chair: I will take equal time with both of them. Look—even the most accomplished stylist can't rush a precision haircut. If your hairstylist has you in and out in twenty minutes, rest assured that even if you're on time for all your other appointments, you're being cheated in the beauty salon. It takes me a long time to cut your hair, so that it will take you twenty minutes to get out in the morning.

Expect a firm, knowledgeable opinion—and the courage born of convictions. The best stylists are not cowed by what you think you want. I will always listen to your thoughts, but even if it means I might lose you as a client, I won't give you Diane Sawyer's haircut—*unless* it's right for you. Sure, you can borrow the style of a celebrity. Every couple of years there are a few stars who launch a thousand haircuts, who inspire women to run to their beauty salons clutching the latest Jennifer Aniston/Farrah Fawcett/Demi Moore photo, and unskilled stylists will give them just that, someone else's look—what the clients *think* they want. Almost always, though, these clients will leave disappointed. They have what looks like the star's hair, but where's Jennifer/Farrah/Demi? In Hollywood, that's where, not in their mirrors. So be realistic about *your*self: Although it's smart money to get ideas from other women, blindly choosing a style just because it looks good on another won't do it for the Big City Look. You need to consider your *own* hair texture, skin coloring, and face shape to get your best look.

Your master stylist should understand individuality and gently discourage you from making a major, hat-on-for-a-month mistake.

Two Big Big City Basics

Eccentricity should be temporary. The woman with the truest Big City Look rarely has outrageous hair. You know what I mean, like the style that originated with the Broadway show *Grease:* sleeked back with the big tuft in the front. One of my colleagues calls that look "trailer-park chic." Fool around with the eccentric hair for a day or so when you're in an eccentric mood, but don't ask your stylist to do anything drastic and unfixable in the cut. Most women with The Look enjoy classic hairstyles, rendered with a touch of individuality.

Consider the city. Even though there is a great deal of overlap, the Big City Look in hair will appear somewhat different in different regions of the country. Lady Godiva would not have made a big hit in Atlanta—all that hair in all that heat! The beautiful hair of a sophisticated woman walking the Magnificent Mile in Chicago will be subtly different from that of a sophisticated woman on Rodeo Drive in Los Angeles. What is chic and appropriate in Dallas society will not automatically work in D.C. or New York.

THE CITY CODES: HAIR

Before I begin to teach you the specific tricks of the hair trade, you must crack the code of the Big City Look in your neck of the woods. It can't be said too often: Swell looks can overlap from city to city, region to region, but there are very specific differences in what looks *most* swell in different parts of the country. For example: In every part of the country, many women opt for the popular hairstyle known as a bob. A Chicago bob, however, is worlds apart from an Atlanta bob, and neither is the same as a New York bob. To recognize the differences, you must get a sense of the chic woman in each particular region.

Cracking the Southern Code: The Look of Atlanta Hair

Atlanta's Code Words: Southern Comfort. The stand-out woman with the Big City Look from this Scarlett O'Hara city (and points south) is a lady. She's feminine in the sweetest *and* strongest sense of the word. Make no mistake: She's not a pushover.

"Remember *Steel Magnolias?*" says Mitchell Barnes, co-owner with Carey Carter of the Carter Barnes Salons in Atlanta. "An Atlantan beauty would never hang up the phone without saying 'Have a good day—come see us,' but she's the same woman who would chew off your head if you displeased her and would *still* expect you to open the door when she's ready to get out of the car."

Charm is her heritage, and the woman with the Atlanta Big City Look moves slowly, almost languidly, through her life. She paces herself to the beat of a city that is considerably less frantic than New York or Washington, D.C. Here in the near tropical heat, clothing is light and cool, and hair is light and cool also, cut and colored with an eye to defense against destructive elements—whether the sun, the pool, or even natural perspiration. At work or play, hair that is *designed, coiffed, stiff* doesn't get A's in Atlanta.

"Blondes are everywhere in Atlanta," says Carter, "and the unwritten credo of the woman with The Look is 'Touch up my roots before you bury

The dressed-up Big City Look in Atlanta might include some added hairpieces for glamour or nostalgia. The nape-of-the-neck braid is always elegant, and the Scarlett O'Hara curls are fun for the ball.

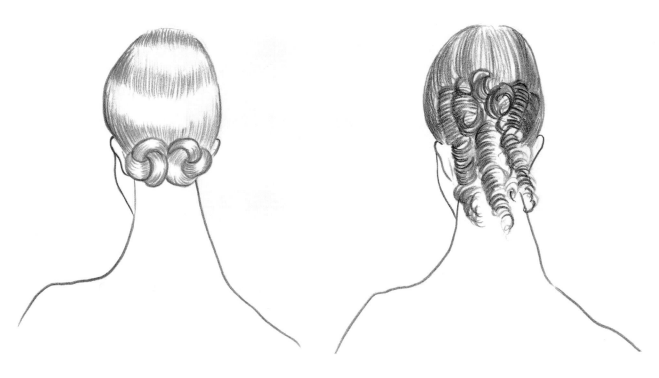

me.' She's got a controlled, simple, classic hairstyle and drawers filled with cute little headbands, scrunchies, and clips to keep it smooth. An Atlanta woman will have a coronary if one hair is out of place!

"Hair spray is a southern woman's friend," adds Carter. "Light mousses to build body are also pals, as are hair polishers with a silicone instead of oil base, which are widely used to get rid of the little flyaways. A strong, clarifying shampoo used once a week in addition to a daily, milder shampoo is necessary to wash everything off. As you can see, there's a lot to wash off."

Here's an interesting statistic: The area of the country where women are most likely to use home permanent kits, giving themselves about three home perms a year, is the South. These do-it-at-home women may have curly hair, but I suspect they do *not* have The Big City Look. Great perms are almost always professionally done.

The number one daytime hairstyle in Atlanta is the classic bob, hair cut one length, just below the shoulder or at the chin. "If it's layered," says Carter, "she's from out of town." The beautiful Kim Basinger, "a big, old southern girl," as someone described her, did layer that bob and let it grow long, but only when she left town. Extremely short, very gamine or pixie styles are also big. Another style you see everywhere on those astonishingly *sportive* Atlanta women is the pulled-back ponytail: no bangs, no fringe, no nothing, just glossy, sleek, wonderful hair caught in black velvet ribbons, suede scrunchies, or shell barrettes—whatever looks most terrific. And in the evening? Those Atlanta beauties sweep up that hair and go out to play. They know how to do that well.

"I can always spot an Atlanta woman in New York," says Barnes. "She's put together in a very conservative, Talbot's sort of way, no Dolce & Gabbana, please. Her jewelry is real and her fragrance is authentic Chanel No. 5—not even Lagerfeld's top of the line. Where New York women try everything as soon as it comes out, taking a 'dare me' attitude, the Atlanta woman looks at everything, then ends up underdone."

These big city hair looks are often seen on the Atlanta knockout:

Toppings. Because the powerful southern sun is a strong bleaching agent, the woman with The Look is often seen with a colorful designer scarf protecting her hair (think Hermès) or just the cutest brimmed tennis

Perfectly feminine yet perfectly powerful, native-born Atlanta businesswoman Sharon Sadler on her terrace overlooking the city. Sharon's wearing a finely elegant chocolate jersey shift that can go to the club, the tea dance, or the theater. Her fine-spun hair is immaculately coiffed—no wild and windswept looks for Atlanta. (Photograph © Denis Reggie)

cap, whether she plays or not. The absolute *cutest* has a hole cut out for her ponytail.

Chunks. In most cities, if you ask for highlights or lowlights you'll get subtle brighteners. But in Atlanta, if you want what used to be called streaks, you ask for "chunks," which are lowlights on one side of a strand of hair and highlights on the other, creating dark/light effects. They're very popular in Atlanta because they mimic the work of the sun. Only in this climate and with lighter hair can they look dramatic and still elegant. You've seen chunks before. Brooke Shields, for example, plays with chunks periodically.

Waves. A short cut with long layers around the face combines the romantic effect of softly dipping waves with the ease of short hair.

Color. For blondes, the southern big city color should be lighter, warmer, *wheatier.* For brunettes, it's less raven-haired brunette and more sun-kissed auburn. Redheads, pick a hue, any hue—that of Tori Amos, Priscilla Presley, Julia Roberts, Wynonna Judd, Nicole Kidman, Reba McEntire. Whatever the hair shade, always think *strong* Georgian sun. What would it do to your particular hair?

Probably the biggest problem in Atlanta, says Carter, is fading caused by the sun. Hair gets red or brassy, so one of the biggest-selling products is a shampoo with a little color pigment added. L'Oreal makes a good one called I'Ridiance; another is Artec. The color shampoos replace the color molecules lost to the sun, humidity, and pool chlorine. The shampoos also keep gray hair crystal clear and blond hair blond.

SPECIAL EFFECTS

- *Weather.* The region has temperatures of seventy to ninety-plus degrees and 70 percent humidity almost daily. Hair products containing sunscreen, vitamins, and natural cleansing agents to counteract the effects of the atmosphere are everywhere.
- *The look of health.* No exotic, Kabuki-type makeup ever looks right in Georgia's capital city, and the same goes for exotic hairstyles—even in the evening. Simple is the watchword—simple and expensive.
- *Tara effect.* Long Scarlett O'Hara tresses from a bygone era? In Atlanta, you could get away with it.

Cracking the Midwest Code:
The Look of Chicago Hair
(and Points Midwest)

Code Word? Real. Chicago is the city of the big shoulders.
The Big City Look in the Midwest hinges on *earthy, spontaneous,
unpretentious:* The lovely-looking woman who makes you stare in Chicago
often has hair that looks as fine and natural as wind-blown wheat.
Chicagoans don't give a hoot about faddish hairstyles. What they like is
honest. Why? It has to do with that wind. The northwest wind really rules
in midwestern states like Illinois—why do you think Dorothy wore braids?
In Chicago, the Big City Look depends on not expecting your hair to stay
put in esoteric designs.

Hair spray hasn't a hope of holding in an Illinois windstorm. Thus,
short but not too cropped, and spontaneous, not-too-styled hair is the key
to the code.

Hair spray aside, the most ubiquitous Chicago hair product, says
Charles Ifergan, owner of the famed Charles Ifergan Hair Salons in
Chicago, is a mousse or a gel that doesn't make hair into a helmet but still
gives it body so that the wind doesn't flatten it. Try Jheri Redding
Volumizer Mousse, Volumac Mousse, or Phytovolume Actif, available in
beauty supply stores. In the wintertime, when Chicago women live mostly
inside because of the killing cold, there's a tremendous amount of static
electricity in the air. Mousse also coats the hair and reduces the flyaway
effect of the electricity.

"The wind always wins," says Ifergan, "so we must work around the
wind. A large part of our clientele lives and works along the lakefront,
where wind is really ferocious. These chic women need a style that easily
returns to itself when the wind blows their hair in every direction. Thus, the
most popular cut here is not an all-one-length bob but a graduated, layered, and bulk-lightened bob that's impervious to wind. The ends, unlike in
a regular bob, aren't heavy and sharp but soft. We develop this style by
what we call a 'fracture cut'—taking chunks inside the hair and cutting
them a bit shorter. When the wind blows our kind of bob, the hair ripples
and waves—like our lake."

In this big city—actually, in any midwestern city—hair, along with
fashion and makeup, really has to be down-to-earth. Real is what's sexy;
real is what works while you're driving the carpool, chairing the board
meeting, coaching Little League, throwing a dinner party, or playing the

clarinet in one of Chicago's many jazz spots. It is interesting to note that when a Chicago woman leaves home, she always retains a kernel of that down-to-earth beauty. As exquisite and glamorous as Cindy Crawford is, look deeply and you can see her down-home, natural Chicago earthiness.

There is an exception to the "real" rule: when the sun goes down. Even though a spontaneous look is de rigueur during the day, sometimes more sculpted styles are knockouts at night, when you're outside for just a few moments between the car and the door and don't have to battle the elements. The woman with the midwestern Big City Look knows how to take the time-less styles of yesteryear and invest them with late-nineties elegance. One Chicago attorney I know can't take his eyes off his wife's hair, which is flat-waved and pincurled at the nape of her neck in a very now version of the twenties flapper style.

And, says Charles Ifergan, "I don't know when you last looked, but the Chicago woman, once so Pilgrim-plain, has become very sensual. At night she's very playful with her hair—often piling it up high, with irre-sistible tendrils escaping."

Chicago color? "We used to be a bright, twenty-four-carat-blond city in the midwestern tradition," says Ifergan, "but as we approach the millen-nium, Chicago is toning down to rich mahoganies and chocolates and deep, flowing ambers, which look so delicious in the late-night hours. When it comes to hair, warm earth tones rule in the Windy City."

Cracking the Mid-Atlantic Code: The Look of Washington Hair

Code Word? Understated. Politics reigns in Washington, D.C., an eastern city with a southern flavor only a stone's throw across the river from Virginia.

The Big City Look here reflects stunning seriousness in hairstyle—except when you're out on your sailboat on the Chesapeake and you can let your hair down. Hair has been important in D.C. ever since the days of George Washington's pigtailed and powdered wig. The premillennium look is definitely lower profile. Urban nonchalance and minimalism are the buzzwords.

"It's an unforgiving town," says one attractive lawyer, her voice becoming lower as she explains. "Your reputation is everything. You wouldn't dare to risk it with the way you did your hair."

Windproof hair (perfect in Chicago or New York) on actress Joanna Kerns.

Sure, Washington, D.C., beauties want more attention paid to what they say than how they look—but make no mistake, they know it always takes a bit of artifice to get out the vote. Artifice in D.C. lies in the new "simple chic." The popular look is an edited look: very simple hair, very simple shoes, simple—but not so simple that it's not worthy of a compliment.

What exactly is The Look in this part of the country? Forget fussy and kiss complicated good-bye when it comes to D.C. hair. Haircuts must be capital cuts—and that's more than a pun. Lester Katz, owner of the famed Washington salon S/P/ALON, says, "Our clients are lawyers, lobbyists, and advocates who like their hair to be conservative but not stiflingly so. They want hairstyle to match lifestyle, which may be trendy but is always tame on the surface. Hair must be easy to deal with during the long workaholic days and into the business/work evenings. The most popular look," says Katz, "is a variation of the classic bob, bluntly cut in layers, or in a slightly elevated version, stacked up in the back or sides to give a sense of fullness. It's groomed and smart-looking, yet relaxed and never messy. Hair must always look smooth, healthy, and shiny in appearance."

You'll also see hair that's clipped superclose at the nape, gradually getting lengthier at the crown—a stunning look that broadcasts serious savvy. You'll see smooth and sleek chignons; you'll see forties "power rolls"; and on the young, you'll see high, glazed ponytails—the ultimate backlash against big hair. About that big hair: You'll not see it anywhere, says Katz, just as you won't see spiked up-dos, or frizzies, or bowl-cut, or waist-length, or heavily frosted hair, or even curly perms on the woman with the fabulous Big City Look in Washington, D.C.

Products? Gels, which add shine and holding power, and sparingly used pomades, which add texture, gloss, and control, are big in D.C. A popular gel here is TG Gel Gloss, and a good styling pomade is Texture Shine, both available in beauty supply stores. Murray's Superior Hairdressing Pomade (call 800-448-6548 for information on local distribution) is another good product.

And color? Women in Washington, says Katz, do like color, but never so dramatic as their New York counterparts. Still, most women at least cover their gray, and many add lots of highlights.

The stunning D.C. woman has just the right briefcase, just the right shoes—low-heeled, and in the finest, softest leather—and she works hard to achieve just the right low-key hair to match.

Two blond chicks in identical Washington bobs dishing the dirt: Liz Smith and Hillary Rodham Clinton.
(Photograph © Jill Lynne)

TWO BITS OF D.C. ADVICE

• Washington is a famously transient town attracting temporary residents from all over the world. When you come to Washington, says Katz, put your hometown regional hairdos on hold, put away your hot rollers and curling irons, and get used to styling with fat Velcro rollers and round brushes for a smooth, more natural, more sophisticated look.

• Washingtonians love formal evening events. Inaugural balls, winter parties, and charity events at the Kennedy Center are constants in the life of the chic woman. The party season usually runs from October into December and even January. Find a more formal hairstyle to separate the day 'do from the night 'do. There are many options, but I love a classic French twist, softened by a few errant tendrils, or even just the classic bob raised at the sides with combs—clear crystal for blondes, tortoiseshell for brunettes—to give extra height and a dash of glamour.

City shades bestow
ATTITUDE!

Cracking the Western Code:
The Look of Los Angeles Hair

L.A. Code Word: Glamour. The woman with the Big City Look in L.A. has a simple code word: glamour.

She's lithe, happy, and straight-backed. She's probably wearing low-cut jeans and oversize shades, and she may have a bottle of Evian water in a designer carrying case slung over her shoulder. She tosses her hair almost imperceptibly every time she wants to make a point. Her hair may have that uncoiffed look, her makeup may *seem* minimal, but make no mistake: Glamour in L.A. is about illusion as much as it is about prettiness, because L.A. is movieland. Illusion takes work.

But here anything is possible—and in hair that includes scrunched Nicole Kidman ringlets, Winona Ryder crops, and classic California hair à la Goldie Hawn—straighter, longer, wilder, more extravagant, more shiny, more swinging than anywhere else in the country.

We're talking blond, bottle blond, *very* blond in L.A.: golden, straw-

Who can forget Janet Leigh in *Psycho?* Still rivetingly lovely, she's got that L.A. Big City Look: dramatic and iconoclastic and very, very blond. Gown by Don Loper.

berry, or platinum Jean Harlow–ish blonds, or Madonna/Evita lemony blonds, or scrubbed girl-next-door blonds. Of course one sees elegant brunettes, too—deep chestnut to warm auburn—and they often have dramatic pixie cuts like Halle Berry's—so, well, *Hollywood*.

California hair often seems God-given. Trust me—it's not. Some do still have the color they were born with, but most stunning L.A. women have highly processed but expertly managed hair, belied by a natural appearance. Polls say that California is the American region where women are most likely to color their hair. Extreme color styles may come and go as fads and may be seen in this neck of the woods, but they never epitomize the true Big City Look. Do-it-yourself color and cut do *not* do it for the sophisticated look others want to emulate. If you're wise, have color and cut done by a professional. Since many L.A. women have color-treated hair, a great conditioner is Paul Mitchell's The Detangler (available in beauty supply shops, or call 800-321-JPMS). Another product to try is René Furterer Okara Rebalancing Shampoo for Color-Treated Hair (call 800-522-8285 for purchasing information).

Protection from the sun is the never-ending quest: I love a moisturizing sun gel and a protective sun oil spray, both called Phytoplage, which provide natural plant-based protection. The gel is for use during and the oil for use after sun exposure. Estée Lauder puts out many wonderful sun-protection products for hair. Ask for them at good department stores.

Cracking the Eastern Code: The Look of New York Hair

New York City's Code Word: Eclectic. That means anything goes! Throw out the hair spray—or, on second thought, keep it, in case you want to try something new that needs holding power! More precisely, anything goes that's dramatic but not gauche or gaudy; traditional but not boring. Never boring. And never silly.

New York women are the first to try out a new hair trend and the first to discard it. Here, women seem to feel most free to develop their own iconoclastic hairstyles and are often willing to look more interesting than pretty. The daring New York woman reads the beauty magazines—and then breaks all the rules. It's easier to pull off more "edgy" trends in New York than in Washington. No one pays much attention if you catch your hair in a topknot with not one but three Chanel barrettes. Nobody even pays much attention if your hair is green—although that's not my idea of a

pretty Big City Look.

Bottom line: The haircut that's everywhere on stunning New York women seems to be a short, feathered bob whose texture comes from short layers that are styled to fall at slightly different lengths around the face. Or it may be swept back from the face, if the mood changes. It's charming and chic at the same time and takes five minutes for the busy New York woman to blow-dry and style.

The weather here is anyone's guess and changes from minute to minute. If your hair is fine and rather straight, it can flatten out to pancake dimensions in humidity. Try Phytovolume Actif (call 800-557-4986 for information) or Aveda Volumizing Tonic (call 800-283-3224 for information). Both give the hair volume without diminishing movement. Apply to wet hair and follow with a blow-dry. For thick, wavy, or extra-curly hair, try a product called Sebastian Laminates Concentrated before blow-drying (call 800-829-7322 for information). And to style very tousled, weather-sensitive hair, try Phytoplage oil—it keeps those curls perfect!

Watch for these Big City Looks in New York, where fashion often takes a walk on the wild side:

- A stunning woman's ruler-straight long hair *streams* out from under a helmet when she rides her mountain bike along Park Avenue. If you see her the next day, that hair might well be bouncing, ringlet-laden on her shoulders when she strides through Central Park with her wheaten terrier. How does she *do* that? Only she knows because . . . anything goes.

- A Belgian-loafered society matron laden with Saks shopping bags draws admiring stares with her stunningly classic, smooth, pageboy-ish bob, but her high-top-sneakered companion also draws approving glances with a heavily textured, quirky crop. What are these two women doing together, anyway? Well, it's New York, isn't it? Anything goes.

- A glimpse of Sigourney Weaver, maybe Isabella Rossellini, window-shopping on Madison Avenue is more than probable: See the highlights in their glorious, romantic hair. Be discreet—don't ask for autographs. *Almost* anything goes—but not autographs. This is New York, right?

The woman who can decipher the New York City code knows to use wooden combs during the day, not rhinestone-encrusted flashers, when she piles her hair high on her head. She knows, like Carolyn Bessette Kennedy does, that a tortoiseshell headband on her honey-colored straight locks is more sophisticated than a colored-cloth version.

The New York woman with the look has her ways of catching a glint of urban gold. She does it *in* her hair. Her brunette locks are dabbed with soft caramel lowlights, her blond tresses capture the gold in sunny nuances. It's glint she's after, not headlights.

Finally, she knows that in New York, it's not considered flaky to be a chameleon. One day she can draw admiring looks from colleagues at work with an asymmetrical part and a wild shag. The next day, with a mood change, she can successfully change her style to a severely stunning, middle-parted bun. How does she know? She just does.

Hair caught high on her head, tendrils escaping, the New York woman radiates easy, fashionable style.

Cracking the Southwest Code:
The Look of Dallas Hair

Code Word: Rich. When we think Southwest, we traditionally think of states like New Mexico or Arizona. Actually, though, Texas, commonly called a central state, is the very *hub* of the Southwest, with influences and roots reaching far into the South *and* the West. The woman with the Dallas Big City Look likes long hair and is quick to point out that her style—particularly *hair*style—is more theatrical than the quieter looks of her sister in Austin, Texas.

There seem to be two cultures in this city, new-guard Dallas and old-guard Dallas—although they often overlap. In new-guard Dallas, a lot of hair, especially big hair, is allowed in the chicest circles, and that doesn't happen in most other cities. This is oil-heiress territory, and the young Texas beauty has hair that's as substantial as her dad's portfolio—as her *own* portfolio. Big hair has gotten a bad rap. It can be terrific-looking when done well with lots of volume, lots of body (mousse is everywhere), and lots

On her terrace with a Dallas backdrop, Beth Decluett is in casual mode. Her hair, beautifully long and full, can grow "big" on a whim. Sadie the dog is never in casual mode. (Photograph © James Richter)

of movement. Texas is synonymous with BIG. This big Big City Look has been popularized by stars like television's *Nanny*, Fran Drescher, Sandra Bullock, Diana Ross, and Texas's own socialite, Lynn Wyatt.

Like it or not, big hair calls for teasing and hair spray—is that an ozone hole over Dallas?—both applied with a subtle hand. In Dallas, says a recent *Allure* magazine beauty poll, 75 percent of the women use hair spray! I like a controlling spray that protects a fuller shape without stickiness. Clairol's Herbal Essences Hair Spray and Paul Mitchell's Firm Super Clean Extra Holding Spray give a nonsticky hold. Phytolaque Medium Hold Botanical Hair Spray also holds hair without weighing it down with sticky glop, as does L'Oréal's Coiffure Tec Ni Lift Mousse—a wonderful volumizer. Kiehl's Creme with Silk Groom is a product from one of New York's top cosmetic pharmacies, but it's perfect for Dallas as well. This product, in every hairstylist's arsenal, gives the hair that "just brushed" touch of volume, texture, and sheen. (Call Kiehl's Since 1851, Inc., 800-543-4572, to order it by mail.)

Here's a tip for subtly sprayed hair: Don't spray directly on your hair but instead spray the bristles of your brush from about two feet away. That controls the electricity in your hair and increases the hair's holding power while still allowing it to bounce. If you must spray directly, hold the can about eight inches from your head.

Not everyone with the Dallas Big City Look has big hair. The Dallas knockout may be a part of the Dallas old guard, a coterie of outdoorsy, upper-crust blondes and brunettes, often with short cuts, one that graduates from ear length in front to collar length in the back or the classic gentle flip—and don't forget the hair spray. Old-guard Texas women often wear their diamonds in the daytime with their tennis or golf togs and wouldn't step out the door without their lipstick, even though their hair is more natural-looking and, yes, somewhat smaller than that of their new-guard counterpoints.

Color? "We love to follow the influence of the land," says a gorgeous old-guard leader. "I mean brunettes who are chestnut and hazel browns rather than the color of licorice; I mean golden blonds—not the brashness of canaries, but dull, soft-polished gold."

SOME TEXAN TOUCHES?

- Green leaves woven into a twist at the nape of the neck.
- A pretty hairnet—yes, a hairnet!—or an Evita-type snood securing a shiny bun.

- A delicate ribbon woven into a glamorous upsweep.
- A hairpiece snuggled into natural hair to give instant volume.
- An evening tiara on a long bob. Can you carry it off?

GETTING STARTED: VINCENT'S THEORY OF RELATIVITY

Einstein's Theory of Relativity, expressed in the formula $E = MC2$, has a lot to be said for it. Little did the gentleman with the crazy white hair know that if he had only used his brilliant formula on his own hair, it wouldn't have looked nearly so crazy. An adaptation of his formula works astoundingly well for me. To find the best formula for your own big city hairstyle, use my version of the theory of relativity: $S = TC3$. Translated, this comes down to:

Style = Texture × Cut, Color, and Care

City style is always a matter of relativity. The elements of style must be related.

The first element to be considered is hair texture.

The second element is the three Cs: cut, color, and care. Combine texture (the first element) with cut, color, and care (the second element), and you have the makings of big city style. Each element must relate to the other; a hairdresser who gives you a cut without considering texture, color, and care won't produce the look you're after.

What's the Texture of Your Hair?

You sit down in the chair of a highly recommended stylist, and before cutting your hair, the expert asks you about your hair texture: "Does it take a tight set? Does it hang limply only two hours after styling?"

What information about your individual hair texture *do* you give the expert before you both decide on a cut? Here's what you should know in order to discuss your best possible look:

The texture of your hair is determined by the *consistency* of the hair, the *amount* of hair on your head, and the *shape* of the individual strands of hair on your head. You have anywhere from ninety thousand to one hundred forty thousand hairs on your head. They may be coarse or fine, curly or straight, thick or thin.

A *thick* head of hair means you've got lots of hairs on your head—even though each individual hair might be thin. A *thin* head of hair means hairs are more sparsely distributed—even though each individual hair might be fat.

Perhaps you'll tell the new stylist that you have a coarse, thick head of hair and that it frizzes like Little Orphan Annie's at the first sign of humidity. Perhaps you'll tell him you think your hair is thin because it hangs limply, even after a body wave. Here's what you need to know about your hair texture and, if you hate it, what you can do to change it.

ALL ABOUT TEXTURE

You have coarse-textured hair if
- your hair resists taking a smooth curl, even with electric rollers.
- your ponytail feels substantial.
- it's difficult to style as you blow-dry.
- it's often bushy, unmanageable, and wild-looking.
- it seems dull, even right after a shampoo.
- humidity is the enemy.

You have fine-textured hair if
- it droops soon after a set.
- it hangs limply or frizzes up when the weather is humid.
- it flys away easily and drives you nuts with static electricity.
- it clings to your face when you wake up.
- your ponytail does not feel substantial.

You have medium-textured hair if
- your hair is dependable—that is, it seems to do the same thing most of the time, depending on how you style it.
- it usually holds a set reasonably well, even if, like all hair, it doesn't look its best if you're tired or stressed or have your period.
- you left your hair dryer home, your hair would still dry naturally with controlled bounce and volume.

What to do if you *hate* your hair texture?
All is not lost. Perhaps your cut and hairstyle would be enhanced

with a change of hair texture. Hair that is too fine, too coarse, too curly, too thin, or too thick literally changes its texture as a result of curling, straightening, or coloring methods. It's not engraved in stone that you have to live with your hair texture if it makes you unhappy.

Changing the Texture by Curling

In this century, perms have come as far as space travel—and that's a very long way. Forget the Shirley Temple curls, the Brillo corkscrews, or the Gibson Girl waves of yesteryear. Custom-designed, beautifully soft and natural perms are available, changing the look and feel of your hair exactly *how* and *where* you need the changes. Example: You can have a permanent just at the tips of your hair and leave the entire crown area straight. And you don't have to wear a paper bag over your head until the perm "relaxes": I defy anyone to detect a permanent even on the day my client has one.

Only a skilled stylist is able to determine how much time is needed to achieve the type of curl the client wishes. Doing it yourself or allowing an unskilled stylist to get his hands on your hair may result in underprocessed hair with curls that relax too soon or overprocessed hair that is too frizzy or curly. By the way, in case you were wondering, the larger the rod, the wider the wave, the bigger and looser the curl.

PERM LINGO

Root perm. The new growth of hair is curled loosely close to the scalp to get extra lift without kinkiness.

Spot wave. This perm gives height and/or curls right at the crown.

Body wave. A looser permanent giving lighter and fuller volume by the use of wider, thicker rods.

Changing the Texture by Straightening

We rarely straighten the whole head of hair anymore, but instead work with a process called "hairline relaxing." It involves a chemical treatment to relax just the frizzies around the face and smooth the outer surface of the entire head of hair. If, however, the hair is very kinky, a total chemical treatment is still an option.

After you have discussed the texture of your hair with the hairstylist, you're ready to discuss a new cut.

BEFORE: Amy Yamaguchi does not make the most of her dramatic possibilities.

DURING: First we cut her hair, keeping it blunt and straight as she wishes, but making it manageable.

AFTER (*right*): French braiding the hair at the crown and using the short hairs around the face as soft, wispy tendrils, we catch the hair in an elastic-covered band and let it do its natural, glossy, shiny thing. A little makeup doesn't hurt, either.

The First of the Three Cs: The Best Cut

Styles hold up only if the cut has provided a foundation for that style—much as a brick house needs a foundation that is made of brick, not mashed potatoes. Suppose you go to your hairstylist, tell him your hair texture is coarse and curly, and ask him to give you a blunt bob—a haircut, either long or short, with a straight-edge line. This is a mistake, because if you give a coarse, mass-of-curls head of hair a blunt cut, it won't hold its blunt shape and will end up looking bushy. On the other hand, fine, thin hair loves a perfect, blunt cut straight across the ends. It gives the hair more bulk.

ALL ABOUT CUT

What do you—and I—need to know about giving you a great haircut, one that's a cut above every other cut you've had? In addition to paying attention to cut as it relates to hair texture, we both need to pay attention to face shape. Please don't ask me to make you look like Sharon Stone if your face is round and the texture of your hair falls most naturally into a tight cap of curls, or like Julia Louis-Dreyfus on *Seinfeld* if your face is square and the texture of your hair is stick-straight and thin. Reality check here. If a sophisticated haircut is to be the end result, I need to rely on my own good

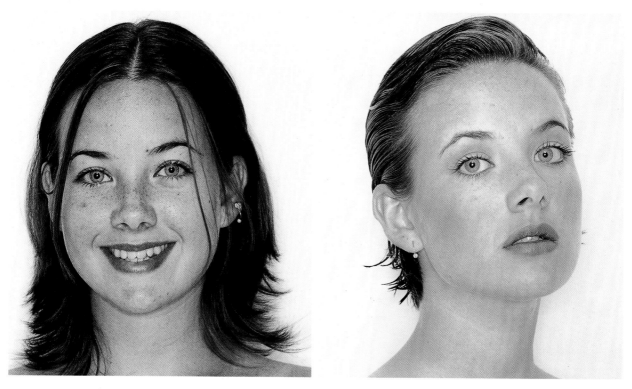

BEFORE: No question, this is a fresh-faced, darling young woman.

AFTER: But with proper and gentle makeup, her hair cut in a layered bob that frames her face, long bangs that can be gelled back or swept back, she is an irresistible knockout!

instincts, experience, and good eye, as well as on your thoughts and the photographs you bring to illustrate the style you're interested in.

In the following section I offer my judgments on the best precision cut for the texture of your hair and then for four classic face shapes: oval, square, round, and long.

Cut and Hair Texture

In the preceding pages, you've identified your hair texture. Now let's focus on the best cut for that texture.

If your hair is medium to coarse, straight, and very thick:
Have it layered for the best flow. Hair that's layered is trimmed in levels that lie smoothly on top of one another, creating fullness and body without the umbrellalike bulk that gives a bushy and unkempt appearance. The layering will dramatize the thickness and quality of your hair, lending a liquid-like movement. Avoid a blunt, all-in-one cut that will make it stand shapelessly away from your face.

You really must have your medium-textured hair shaped regularly. Otherwise, when it grows out, it will look bushy. During this process, ask

Actress Anne Archer (*Fatal Attraction, Patriot Games*) has wonderful medium-textured, straight hair. She can find a totally new look and go from savagely wild to sensual in a moment simply by pulling her hair up with a grip comb. Layering is the answer. (Photograph © Nancy Ellison)

your stylist not to use a razor or thinning scissors to reduce the thickness: Bulk is better reduced by cutting the hair on an angle, in layers. You might consider the softest of body waves applied only to the base of the hair shaft, because that's the trouble spot, the area that first goes limp.

If your hair is coarse, straight, but not very thick:
Opt for a blunt, all-one-length cut to show off hair movement and quality without giving it too much width or a bushy appearance. Sleek, blunt cuts on long or short hair make the hair *move*—think of that gorgeous, blunt-cut Asian hair you've always admired.

If your hair is already layered, it might need a gentle root perm, to give controlled volume. This is why you're better off with a blunt cut, which will never need a perm.

If your hair is coarse and curly:
For those little ringlets that go every which way, choose a short, layered style, which will give a pretty, wind-blown look. Your hair should be cut *with* the natural curl, not against it. Ask your stylist to shape it dry, so he can get an idea of how it will react to a pair of scissors. If coarse, curly hair is cut for the first time when wet, the stylist doesn't get a chance to see just how much or in what direction it will crimp up when dry. After the hair is blow-dried, more can always be cut off; that's better than taking off too much, too soon.

If your hair is silky fine and straight, but kind of thick:
A blunt, chin-length cut with straight-across bangs will look terrific. A few graduated longer layers cut around the crown will give volume. Your hair's natural thickness will compensate for the fineness if it's cut properly, and it will *move*! If your hair is very short, you will probably need to have it more seriously layered for volume.

If your hair is fine and thin:
Your hair will definitely look better short, in a blunt cut. It will need a permanent wave or body wave added to the blunt cut to give fullness. The weight of long fine hair pulls the hair down and makes it seem to have even less body than it has.

If your hair is fine and curly:
Your best cut is in elongated, not short, layers to add volume. Short layers will cause the hair to stick close to the head in a tight, helmetlike vise. Some soft wisps around the face will give the hair an even fuller appearance. Or why don't you try a curly bob with hair shorter in the back than the front?

For fine, curly hair, bangs are perfect. Cut them thick for high foreheads and wispy and spiked for narrow foreheads. You have a choice with most bangs: brush them forward, or brush them back for a fuller look.

If your hair is medium-textured and straight:
Since layers give volume, I'd try a shorter, slightly layered cut, trimmed in levels that lie smoothly on top of one another. That creates fullness and body without weight to drag the hair down and make it limp. Medium-textured shoulder-length straight hair will also look great layered. An option is to perm just the underneath layer to give more body and still retain the smooth, sleek look of the top layer.

If your hair is coarser-textured and a mass of ringlets:
Although a long, wide mane of curly hair can be just wonderful if your features are perfect, your frame can carry it, and *especially* if you come from Dallas, I think the Big City Look is best served here with a short, layered haircut. Ask your hairstylist to cut *with* the natural curl, not against it. I've recently given this cut to author and political commentator Arianna Huffington, and she looks beautiful. Again, if you're new to the stylist, ask to have your hair shaped a bit when it's dry—just to see how the hair will fall. Then, seeing the direction in which it curls, the stylist can complete the cut with the hair wet. If hair is really frizzy—à la Little Orphan Annie—I love to cut the whole head dry: this hair texture is fabulous in a short, cropped style.

Cut and Face Shape

Just as you pay attention to the texture of your hair before you cut, you should also be aware of the shape of your face; a great-looking cut should also flatter the shape of your face.

What shape is your face? No one has a perfectly oval, perfectly square, perfectly round, or perfectly long face, but everyone comes closer to one of these categories than the others. Here's an easy way to judge your face shape: Pull your hair back with an elastic band or headband so all you see is face—not your hairstyle. Stand close to a well-lit mirror and with a dampened bar of soap slowly trace your face outline onto the mirror. Now you know your face shape! Let's consider which styles most flatter specific face shapes, keeping in mind that there are exceptions, depending on the texture of your hair.

If your face is square:
Of course, having a "square" face does not mean your face is perfectly

Journalist Cynthia McFadden's blunt bob can be flipped under or over with a marvelously versatile cut for her perfectly lovely, perfectly square-shaped face. Contrasting blond highlights in her naturally chestnut hair complement her great cheekbones.

straight at the top and bottom, like a real square, but if it seems broader and more solid at the jaw and forehead and if it seems as wide as it is long, you have a predominantly square face. Think of Maria Shriver, newscaster and wife of Arnold Schwarzenegger; she has a square face. So does news journalist Cynthia McFadden.

You do wonderfully with a full, softly layered hairstyle, perhaps parted in the center. If your face seems equally square at both forehead and jaw, you want to deemphasize and soften the squareness at the chin by keeping hair close to the face at the temples and jawline. The hairline could

32

curve around and under the jaw, thus "rounding out" the points of the square. If your face is squarest at the jaw, ask your stylist to give you a cut that's fuller at the top to deemphasize that jaw. If your face is squarest at the forehead, your hair should be fuller at the jaw and more narrow at the forehead. Note: If you wear bangs, think about medium-length bangs cut slightly shorter in the center. They appear to narrow the forehead and lengthen the center of the face, giving you a more oval shape.

If your face is round:

If your face shows more cheeks than cheekbones, if it's circular and full, it's a round face—no surprise to you. Think of actress and talk-show hostess Rosie O'Donnell: She has a round face. Hillary Clinton's face is also roundish.

You do wonderfully with a longer, layered cut with more height on top, narrowly tapered down the neck and below the chin. Fuller hair that spirals out at the ear and then comes in to hug the neck also serves to narrow your round face.

If you wear bangs, I like them delicately layered with jagged ends creating, visually, an up-and-down movement. Skin should remain visible under the hair, because this will make your round face seem longer. Or you might try asymmetrical bangs swept to one side, which also deemphasizes the round face.

If your face is long, thin, angular:

If your face seems to have a high forehead and a longish chin, if it's defined by great bones and is, on the whole, narrow, you have a predominantly long face. Actress Jamie Lee Curtis has a long, thin face.

You need fullness around the face. If your hair is curly, you're in luck. Otherwise, consider getting a perm. If your hair holds a set nicely, a few Velcro or hot rollers at the side of the face for ten minutes will give you volume that softens angularity. A side part will also seem to widen the forehead. Avoid height and fullness at the top of the head. Note: If you wear bangs, a solid, blunt-cut fringe ending at the brows—maybe a tad below—shortens the high forehead commonly found on a long face. Wisps also soften an angular face and are great especially on a narrow face without a high forehead.

If you have an oval face:

You're blessed among women. If your face is broadest between the ears and slowly tapers to a gentle curve at the top and bottom, you have a predomi-

nantly oval face. News journalist Diane Sawyer has a perfect oval face. Almost any cut that flatters your features and meshes with the texture of your hair is terrific. I think straight hair on an oval face looks fabulous in a short, sharply-angled-at-the-jaw cut. If your hair is very curly, a shorter cut looks most chic. If you wear bangs, consider "scissoring" them. Uneven wisps draw attention to your perfectly shaped face.

A GREAT HAIRCUT

How do you know if you have a great haircut—a style that's just right for you? You know because

- you're not my slave: You don't need me to come to your house in the morning to make your hair pretty.
- after a swim, when you've tousled it gently with your fingers or a brush, it still looks terrific.
- even with fine, limp hair, you should still be able to create some volume.
- you do that thing with your head, and your hair bounces. Or swirls, like a river. What it doesn't do is sit there flat and dead.
- people stop you in the street and say, "I've never done this before but could you please tell me . . . where did you get your haircut?"
- you feel you have that Big City Look.

The Second C:
The Best Color for Your Hair

The options today for color are amazingly varied. Gotta get real here. Color depends on skin tone, yes, but also on lifestyle—do you have the *time* to be a double-process blonde? Anyone—grandmothers, young girls, even women with hair loss—can consider mild to major color changes, if the new color will be appropriate to skin tone and lifestyle.

Even if you have been a natural brunette since you were born, perhaps now that you're forty-seven, that "natural" color isn't terrific for you anymore, because your skin color has definitely changed. Maybe hair just a *hint* of a shade lighter would be more appropriate? Or perhaps you love being a platinum blonde. Everyone at home in L.A. told you you were a

Champagne-blond actress/dancer Wendy Waring (*Will Rogers Follies, Crazy for You*) looks perfect in a point-fringe cut that moves with her moves. Cut with fringed bangs in lots of layers from the crown of the head to the nape of the neck, it can be blow-dried toward her face in about three minutes. When her look calls for sophistication, the same hair can be gelled back behind her ears with stunning effect.

perfect platinum, but you now live and work in Washington, D.C., where the tone is tamer—and platinum works to impress only on credit cards.

ALL ABOUT COLOR

The old barbershop quartets made sure we will always remember Jeannie with the light brown hair, but we'll also never forget Carole Lombard with the platinum hair, Cher and Elizabeth Taylor with the raven hair, Madonna with the . . . *whatever* hair. Hair color identifies us more than anything else.

So how do you know which color will be most wonderful, most Big-City Look–ish for you? *You* really can't know. You have to take an educated guess—then trust the expert. Let's say you were born with Liz's raven hair, but now you're forty-five, and the last time you looked, your hair was quite salt-and-pepperish. Also, your skin is no longer quite the wondrous olive you remember so fondly. Actually, it's faded a bit, truth be told. So you've decided to take the big step and color your hair. Should it be the old raven hair? Definitely not. You can no longer carry raven. Neither can Liz—and she knows it.

What you need is natural-looking color—natural to the way you look now, not the way you looked twenty years ago; color that will make you your prettiest! For beautiful, natural-looking hair at any age, Mother Nature *can't* be trusted. Frankly, and modesty aside, I think I'm a better judge of your best color possibilities than Mother Nature, who often makes mistakes—especially after a certain age, when she almost always opts for gray. You may think you want to be a canary-blonde, but I know that a soft auburn will best bring out your light and radiance. Or you may be only twenty years old, but Mother Nature in one of her cranky moods gave you sixty-year-old mouse-brown hair. "Thank God for chemicals!" is my credo—and it should be yours.

So we must find the right color—and, believe me, we will. Know that natural hair color is not just one color but many subtle shades softly blending. Your own dark hair may include shimmering highlights of auburn, perhaps ash. Your own blond hair may have silver, lemon, or honey lights.

When you change the color of your hair, you need color and highlights that can be duplicated, month after month. It won't do to be red-haired Rita Hayworth one month and platinum Marilyn Monroe the next.

Do It Yourself? I Think Not

It isn't easy. Getting a good color depends on taking into account fading processes, weather conditions, my customer's allergies, even her hormones. I use years of experience to mix a color with subtleties that are consistent with the previous month's color. This means that one day I may leave the hair color on for forty minutes. On another day, on the same customer, the same formula will take only twenty minutes to develop. Go figure. Well, I've figured it. And unless you're a professional, you haven't.

Forrest Gump Wisdom

Home coloring kits usually provide directions instructing the customer not to worry. She's told to leave the color on for, say, forty minutes. If she loses track of the time, no problem: After a certain time the Chestnut Brown (or Champagne or Strawberry Blond) stops deepening.

That's simply not true. Most color just keeps going on and on and on. A home color kit is like a box of chocolates; to paraphrase a hero named Gump: You never know what you're going to get.

What Color for Me?

I really can't know unless you're sitting in my chair, so I can check out your skin color, your eyes, your haircut, your lifestyle, even your body shape. But I *can* give you an idea here of the best hair colors for you on the basis of your eye and skin color. For the final choice, you need to talk it over with your own expert and decide together.

The Eyes Have It

The eyes are a fine barometer of your most stunning and natural-looking hair shade.

If your eyes are a shade of deep brown

Your skin most likely has olive or chocolate tones. Olive skin does not go with really light hair—ever. The hair will look brassy, the skin greenish. Since olive has brown, green, and gray in its mix, try a cinnamon red or a warm auburn to blend with those colors. For you, glamour could also mean a change to deep, coppery brown with a few delicate ginger highlights around the face.

Hardly anyone looks wonderful in jet-black hair. By the same token, hardly anyone looks wonderful in blue, burgundy, or lipstick-red hair. Stick to colors one sees in nature.

If your eyes are a very light brown

Your skin is probably a medium shade, and lush, deep brown hair with warm auburn highlights around the face could be gorgeous. The caveat for

Kathie Lee Gifford's hair is a cinnamon-y red—just right for her sable-brown eyes. She has a *spectacular* N.Y. Big City Look.

everyone to remember: Your hair can be a shade or so lighter than your natural hair color—*but no more than one shade lighter.*

If your eyes are very, very blue or even violet

It's a good bet you have peachy, creamy skin—a natural for those with blue and violet eyes. Since your skin is very fair, sunny golden-blond hair will be beautiful. Think Grace Kelly. If you're under thirty, you'll be smashing in champagne. Think Jean Harlow.

TIP: There are a very few pale-skinned people who look terrific in rich, dark hair. Think Liza Minnelli or the young Liz Taylor. But be careful here; dark hair can seem phony if it's not colored subtly. Also, you might try a lighter, warm, chestnut brown. No red, please. Older, more mature skin matched with robin's egg–blue eyes looks marvelous with cocoa, even sandy-brown hair.

If your eyes are gray-blue or a shade of green

Your skin is also probably very fair. Try honey-colored or baby blond hair with no element of ash added. In fact, no one over the age of twenty-five should ever have ash added to her hair. It makes the skin appear sallow.

If your eyes are hazel (a greenish-brown color)

I've seen women with very fair skin and hazel eyes, but I've also seen those eyes with olive-based skin. Whatever the case, and whatever your age, it's a good bet that deep honey or dark ash-blond are good shades for you. You might also try a caramel brown or a coppery red. Hazel eyes warn you not to go too dark in your hair shade.

   If you have what is commonly recognized as an English or Irish complexion—ruddy, outdoorsy, and often flushed—your natural hair color is probably close to Nicole Kidman's: strawberry blond. If you're young, rejoice and keep that color. If you're older and the color has faded, try some of the paler browns—or you can weave in some rich cognac or tawny color highlights.

Is gray hair always a bore?

You know it isn't. Perhaps you're most comfortable with your naturally gray hair. I can't say I'm thrilled with your decision. Although some women—the model Carmen, for example—do look wonderful with gray hair, I think most are prettier with color added to cover the gray. If you really want to keep the gray, go for it, but make sure your gray is silver-fox gray, not yellowing-newspaper gray.

The Language of Color

"Talk to me," says your hairstylist—and you must. Together, you'll discuss your options for hair color. But, as in any strange country, you have to know the language.

What is a highlight?

A highlight is a color lighter than your own color applied with a tinfoil process. For the most natural effect, the highlighting color should be a few shades lighter than your overall hair color. Gentle streaks of bleach can be carefully strewn through the hair to give a brightening, pretty effect. Blondes look marvelous with lighter, silvery highlights. Brunettes look fine with auburn or reddish, never blond, highlights.

What is a lowlight?

A particularly subtle color highlight—only a little lighter than one's natural color, applied with tinfoil. The end result looks as if the sun kissed your hair.

What is frosting?

Frosting gives an all-over salt-and-pepper effect to the hair by bleaching tiny strands throughout to blend and contrast with the darker hair. Frosting must be subtle if it's not to look garish.

What's streaking?

Larger strands of hair lightened with a brush—much like painting—for more dramatic effect. The streaks must also gently blend in with the overall color.

What are tips?

Some of the *ends* of the hair strands are lightened for contrast.

What is henna?

Henna is a natural vegetable dye. I hate henna and never use it anymore. It puts a coating on the hair that reduces the shine.

What is the tinfoil process?

Color or bleach that produces gentle highlights is applied to small sections of hair. The sections are then wrapped in tinfoil squares to separate them from the rest of the hair, which, before the squares are removed, gives the client the appearance of a space alien.

What is single-process color?

One application of color is placed on the roots of the client's previously colored hair for approximately thirty to thirty-five minutes. If the hair has become oxidized from the sun or the elements, I mush the color through the whole head of hair for the last three minutes.

What is double-process color?

If a client wishes a total makeover—say, to change the hair color from dark brown to blond—the first process consists of totally bleaching out the present hair color. In the second process, the new color is added—and that may include highlights or lowlights. It all takes at least an hour and a half.

If you desire a total change in color and a stylist tells you he can do it in one process, get out of the chair. It cannot be done without a brassy effect resulting. During a single process, the stylist has far less control over the exact shade aimed for. It takes starting from scratch to produce great new color. One caveat: Double-process color does require heavy-duty maintenance on the client's part. This means avoiding the sun (which can change the color and even damage the hair), using excellent conditioners, and appearing for regular touch-ups, which can easily take thirty-five to forty minutes. Black roots peering through sunny hair is never the Big City Look—in any city.

What is permanent and semipermanent color?

"Permanent color" means permanent till the new hair growth appears, which takes three to six weeks. Semipermanent color slowly rinses out in four to six shampoos. It doesn't last long and barely covers gray hair. Since the color fades evenly from the hair, not just from the roots, the one advantage to semipermanent color is that those telltale roots don't show so clearly.

What is a temporary rinse?

A temporary rinse doesn't lighten or darken; it tones. A temporary rinse washes away with the first shampoo. I use it mostly on blondes to tone down the brassiness a beginning stylist gave them.

What in heaven's name is a drabber?

Your hair looks like Lucille Ball's? This product get rids of too much red.

What is color painting?

A skilled stylist can simply brush bleach on in tiny areas for lightening effects. Color painting can be used to visually widen or narrow face shapes.

What is a cream crown?

During any color process, ask your hairstylist to apply a good facial cream around your hairline to keep the color dye from tinting your skin.

COLOR DOS AND DON'TS

DOS

- *Color your brows.* If you're having your hair colored, consider doing the same to your brows, which should be a tad lighter than your hair. Never do this yourself, and only have it done in an extremely reputable salon: There have been too many cases of eye damage arising from inexperienced practitioners.
- *Highlight your dark hair.* Most brunettes think they can't have highlights and still look refined and chic. Brunettes *can* have gorgeous highlights, but they must be pulled off with an extremely subtle hand to avoid the skunk effect.
- *Carry color crayons.* If you're not able to have your hair colored for

a long time—perhaps you're out of the country or you're ill—a color crayon is a great tool to camouflage ugly roots. Roux's Tween Time Crayons or Cover Gray are good products.

DON'TS

- *Don't color it yourself.* Maybe you'll think I'm being self-serving, but please, please, have your color done professionally. Would you set your own broken leg? Today's home coloring kits are safer and more reliable than their predecessors, but they still can't hold a candle to a professional who's trained to see the subtle nuances of your hair. The Big City Look is never served by the unblended licorice blacks, Hershey browns, harsh yellows, and reds that come straight out of a bottle you buy at the drugstore.
- *Don't ask me to give you your color formula.* There's a reason hairstylists never tell customers the private formula for their hair color—it's one of our trade secrets.
- *Don't dye or bleach more than every three to five weeks.* You want to avoid damaged hair, don't you?
- *Don't wash your hair the day, or even the day before, you come to the salon to have it colored.* Everyone does it—God forbid the hairstylist should see you with less-than-squeaky-clean hair. Washing the hair opens the hair shaft and makes you more liable to have an itchy or burning reaction to the color.
- *Don't let your hairstylist dye your whole head of hair each time you meet.* Dye only the new growth. Occasionally, the hairstylist will mush the color all through the hair for the last few moments, then quickly wash the whole head.

The Third C:
The Best Care for Your Hair

Hair care includes washing, drying, conditioning, and nourishing, but care is not the same for everyone. Does your lifestyle dictate only a twice-a-week wash routine? Do you have to wash your hair daily? Once you have determined whether your hair is oily, dry, or medium and what your unique needs are, you'll know what kind of shampoos and conditioners you require.

You have oily hair if

- your hair looks greasy and flat if you don't wash it every single day.
- you suffer from telltale dandruff.

You need to use hair-care products designed for oily hair.

You have dry hair if

- your hair is brittle.
- you often have split ends.
- your hair is flyaway feathery.
- your hair looks dull more often than not.

You need to use hair-care products designed for dry hair.

The section below will help you create the best routine for the prettiest hair in the world.

ALL ABOUT HAIR CARE

How should hair care differ for different people? Very fine hair needs far fewer conditioning treatments than coarse hair. Some hair just doesn't need a daily wash—if you spend your days inside an air-conditioned office, how dirty does your hair get? Those who swim daily must shampoo daily to get rid of the pool chlorine. In fact, swimmers should use a gloppy conditioner to protect their hair before they dream of entering a chlorine-filled public pool. (Here's a little-known fact: The most up-to-date pools use ozone instead of chlorine to treat their pools. Since ozone is much easier on the hair than chlorine, you might look for such a pool.)

With a little advice from your hairstylist, you must be the judge of your own needs. Whatever you do, make sure the end result looks fabulous—or find other products, other care routines. You've never seen a woman with the Big City Look whose hair didn't shine, didn't bounce with health—I guarantee it.

Wash It! The Right Stuff

You pour on any shampoo and conditioner and just scrub—right? Wrong on both counts. Ever notice how your hair *particularly* shines and bounces after a trip to the salon? It's no magic, no accident. They're using the right stuff for your particular hair.

A famous detective once said that there are a million stories in the big city. Well, there are *ten* million hair products in the big city—many of them terrific; more of them not so terrific. I've long admired the Phytologie line of hair-care products. Every time I mention a product that begins with "Phyto," this line is what I'm talking about. (For information on where the products are sold, call 800-557-4986.) The products are light and enormously effective. Made from natural plant extracts, they originate in France but are now readily available at most large department stores as well as in some drugstore chains and beauty salons. In the following sections, I'll also mention other effective products. For the *right stuff* for your hair, read on.

If your hair is oily

You need to shampoo daily, if possible, but each person is different. Sometimes daily washes can activate oil glands, and the more you wash, the oilier it gets. Experiment to find the right formula for your hair. Try any fragrance-free, pH-neutral shampoo. pH is the measure of acidity or alkalinity in hair (which should be slightly acid). Many hair products and treatments leave an alkaline residue on the hair, which can damage it. A pH-neutral shampoo should leave no alkaline residue.

You can also shampoo with Phytoneutre, then follow with a treatment of Phytosaponaria G25. This routine cleanses some oily hair of impurities and excessive sebum, the fatty secretions of the sebaceous glands, which lubricate hair and skin. Origins Clear Head Mint Shampoo is designed for people who do wash their hair daily.

If daily shampoos seem to work well on your oily hair, one method to enhance the oil-removing effects of the shampoo is to wash, rinse, and wash again, leaving the shampoo on your scalp for five minutes before the final rinse. The unfortunate truth is that sebaceous glands are activated each time you shampoo, so it's really difficult to rectify the problem of oily hair. Extremely oily hair responds well to an oil-stripping shampoo, which may or may not contain alcohol. I suggest asking for a good oil-stripping shampoo *without* alcohol in any beauty supply store.

If your hair is dry

You don't have to shampoo every single day; if you do so, you need a shampoo rich in emollients. Try L'Oréal's Hydra-Vive Moisturizing Shampoo or Clairol's Herbal Shampoo. I've also seen extremely dry hair do very well with Phytojoba, a shampoo that seems to hydrate and really revive the hair.

Make sure there's no drying alcohol in any product you use (shampoos, mousses, gels, pomades)—the one exception being hair spray, because it's the alcohol in hair spray that does the holding. If you use a lot of hair spray—are you listening, Dallas?—make sure you also use a clarifying shampoo every week or so; these shampoos are especially formulated to get rid of the product buildup. Phytoapaisant nicely eliminates product residues. Origins The Last Straw Conditioning Shampoo bills itself as being for hair that's "dyed, dried or fried," and it's wonderful. Johnson's Baby

Shampoo is also terrific for removing product buildup.

If you have fine or thin hair

You needn't shampoo daily, but you do need a protein shampoo. There are many on the market, and you can find out about them by asking in a beauty supply store. Think about trying Phytovolume, which coats and swells the hair strands: only use it once or twice a week. Avoid creme rinses like the plague and try an herb-based conditioner like Aveda's Deep-Penetrating Hair Revitalizer.

If you have dandruff

Oh, those embarrassing white flakes! Try Phytocoltar, the best dandruff treatment shampoo I know of, and follow the directions. Some of my clients also swear by a simple shampoo made from pure nonalkaline Castile soap—just what your grandma used to use—available in any beauty supply or health food store. Some of my clients also recommend a product called Meri-Dan (available in beauty supply stores), which has five different dandruff formulas for five different hair types.

If your hair is dandruff-free, neither dry nor oily, neither thin nor bushy

You have normal hair, lucky you. I like Paul Mitchell products or a mild protective shampoo called Phytopanama. Your hair is so good, you can do little wrong by experimenting with any appealing product.

If you have split ends or otherwise damaged hair

Use a shampoo with a low pH and built-in protein conditioners and try to fit in weekly warm oil treatments (see deep-conditioning advice on page 47). The only definitive way to get rid of split ends is to cut them off, but the oil treatments do help. Phytorhum is a good shampoo for stressed and otherwise damaged hair.

Use caution to prevent damaged hair in the future: Keep your hair dryer on medium rather than high, avoid electric rollers, and use a natural-bristle brush with smooth-edged bristles instead of a synthetic brush with rough-edged bristles. Remember that a short hairstyle harbors fewer split ends than long hair.

GENERAL TIPS

- Whatever your hair type, I advise using a great clarifying shampoo every five to six weeks. I mentioned some good ones above. All the big city's grime and smog buildup, hair spray, and other product accumulations need to be removed.

- Avoid always using the same products. Give another product a turn. Hair builds up tolerances to hair products similar to the way the body builds a tolerance to penicillin. I recommend finding three terrific shampoos and three conditioners that work for you and alternating them, week by week, instead of sticking with the same product for years on end.
- Common sense tells savvy and chic women to follow their own rules. They wash their hair when it's dirty. Period.

Condition, Nourish, and Moisturize It!

Show me a woman who doesn't use a nourishing after-shampoo product and I'll show you a woman whose hair doesn't look as wonderful as it could. If your hair is treated chemically, you don't even have a choice. If your hair is really fine and limp, you have to be careful, of course, because most conditioners will make it even more limp. Still, there are conditioning products that coat and reinforce hair fibers, giving limp hair more volume and bounce.

A conditioner by any other name—a creme rinse, a lotion, a detangler—is still a conditioner, to be applied to clean, wet hair after washing. Conditioners come in squeeze tubes, bottles, spray cans, caplets. Some stay on, some wash out, some are thick, some are thin. Experiment to see which works best for you and always follow the product directions to see if the conditioner is to be left on or rinsed off.

If you have coarse, thick, or bushy hair

I suggest that you use a conditioner composed of protein or fibers after each shampoo; I also think that a regular deep-conditioning treatment (described on page 47) is a great boon to hair. Origins Knot Free Finishing Rinse is wonderful for hair that's hard to comb. I also like Phytodefrisant Relaxing Balm, which makes hair far more manageable after shampooing. Don't rinse it out. You might also try another leave-in conditioner called Keragenics Rejuvenating Treatment, to make thick hair behave as if it were thinner.

If you have fine or thin hair

If your hair is fine or thin, consider doing without the conditioner, or use conditioners and styling products containing balsam or resin. These contain body-building properties and offer more holding power to a chosen style. Billed as an "aftershampoo," Phytovolume Actif works like a good conditioner.

If you really love using a conditioner and your hair is *extremely* fine or thin, condition *before*, not after, you wash, for more body.

If you have thin and/or fine hair, you should never opt for leave-in conditioners. They're going to drag down your hair. Try diluting the conditioner with water to cut down on hair limpness.

If you have oily hair

Try Phytosébor, which seems to stabilize the sebum flow and makes the hair bouncier and easier to comb and style. You might also experiment with Paul Mitchell Shampoo Two for oily hair. Finally, one of the best oil-stripping shampoos I know is plain old inexpensive Prell.

If you have dry hair

Try Origins The Last Straw Conditioning Shampoo if your hair seems "dyed, dried or fried." Aveda's Deep-Penetrating Hair Revitalizer is particularly great for moisturizing chemically colored hair (call 800-283-3224 for information on distributors). Phyto 9 is a daily nourishing cream that revitalizes and conditions dry hair without making it limp.

If your hair is stressed

Try a treatment with Phytopolleine, a product that seems to counteract the effects of pollution and stress (too much sun, chlorine, bleach, or salt water) by vitalizing and nourishing. Extremely damaged hair is repaired beautifully by a product called Hi-Pro Pac Conditioner (available at drugstores nationwide). Système Biolage, sold in professional beauty salons, is a great product for stressed hair.

If you need swim salvation

I advise my clients who swim in chlorine-treated pools to use a product that removes any chlorine that penetrated the conditioner barrier they applied before the swim. Chattem Inc.'s Ultraswim Shampoo and Conditioner and Paul Mitchell's Shampoo Three are good choices.

If you want ultimate conditioning

A WARM OIL, DEEP-CONDITIONING TREATMENT

A weekly deep-conditioning treatment is great for chemically treated or sun-damaged hair. It lubricates and softens. Have it done at the salon or do it yourself with warm olive oil. Here's how:

On a low flame, heat about two tablespoons of virgin olive oil. With cotton puffs, apply the warmed oil to hair tips and other areas that seem damaged. Then, using a wide-toothed rubber comb, distribute the oil throughout the hair. Wrap a warmed wet Turkish towel around the scalp, changing it periodically as the towel cools. The warmth opens the hair cuticles and allows the oil to penetrate. This procedure should take about twenty minutes.

Finally, remove the towel, massage the scalp lightly, shampoo, and rinse thoroughly.

VINCENT'S CONDITIONING FORMULA FOR ALL TYPES OF HAIR

Sometimes I call this my high-shine secret. Wash and dry your hair without styling it. Beat three eggs. Apply the eggs all over and through your hair and let them dry on the hair—it takes about forty-five minutes to an hour. When the eggs have dried and penetrated the hair, rinse through with tepid, then cool water. Dry and style. The healthy shine will be blinding!

THE MOST FABULOUS CONDITIONER IN THE WORLD

If you know me, and have seen my multicompartment vitamin box, which travels with me *everywhere*, you know I'm a health nut. Internal nourishment works to condition your hair better than the most expensive product on the market. Whatever you put in your mouth—the Hershey's kisses, the aspirins, the birth-control pills—show up in the appearance of your hair. I guarantee that the woman you can't take your eyes off of because her hair is so spectacular eats plenty of fruits and veggies and enjoys a balanced diet rich in minerals, natural vitamins, proteins, and complex carbohydrates. An occasional glass of fine wine is good for the psyche—thus, also good for the general health and condition of your hair. I beg you: Nourish your body—and nourish your hair. That's the most fabulous conditioner in the world.

Dry It!

But before you dry: This is the best time to apply any of a myriad styling products to give your hair bounce, shine, and hold. Many of these products—even if they're sprays—are best applied by putting a dab between your hands, rubbing your hands together, and then using those hands as combs. Try the following to see which works with your hair:

- *Styling mousse* looks and feels like shaving foam. A lightweight mousse is an indispensable product for adding volume and direction, especially to fine, thin hair. A little goes a long way, and there are dozens of choices on the market. I especially like the mousse put out by Redken because it contains no alcohol. Bain de Terres has another great mousse (call 800-242-WAVE, ext. 7859, for distributor information).

- *Volumizers* are lotions or sprays that coat flat, limp, fine hair to give it a fuller look. Salon Selectives puts out a good "bodyifying" volumizer hair spray—get maximum hold 15.
- *Texturing gels* add body, shape, shine, and volume to hair. Origins puts out a good one called Take Control Stylizing Gel. In the tube version, the gel looks and feels like clear toothpaste. It's available in a spray version.
- *Heat-activated styling spray* is a great new body builder that responds to heat from a dryer or a heated curling product like hot rollers. It's available as both an aerosol and a nonaerosol spray.

HOW TO DRY

Next to the invention of aluminum foil and maybe my homemade pasta e fagiole with a glass of 1973 Bertani Amarone, the blow-dryer is humankind's best discovery. Depending on the shape and size of your brushes or rollers, this tool can straighten *or* curl your hair as it drys it.

- Always towel-dry sopping-wet hair before blow-drying.
- If you wish, now's the time to finger-comb a volumizer or gel through your towel-dried hair.
- There are two ways to blow-dry your hair: using "hair acupuncture" or section by section.

Blow-drying by hair acupuncture

I think I invented the method of using brushes instead of rollers to set hair, but it is seen now in every salon and health club. Why are brushes terrific for hair setting? Wrap hair about a roller and it seems to just lie there. Wrap your towel-dried hair around a round brush and the bristles lock it in—providing a softer, fuller brushout. With the handles jutting out, the brushes make the head look as though it's undergoing an acupuncture treatment. I've been known to saw off the handles of new brushes for a complete set of "brush" rollers, but they're probably easier to use with the handles left intact. Blow-dry the brush-set hair using medium to low temperature—never high. Remove the brushes, brush out, and style. What an extraordinary result!

If the hair gets stuck between the bristles, take the tip end of a tail comb (which has a long, thin, pointed handle), insert it under the hair that's stuck, and pull gently; the hair strands will come loose.

Blow-drying section by section

Hold the blow-dryer five to six inches from your head. Lift hair in sections around a round brush (keeping a gentle tension on the hair) and direct air flow to the roots of the hair as you lift up. This stretches and straightens the hair to a natural curl. The secret to the curl or straightening is drying the roots first—then the hair wrapped around the brush. Don't remove the hair from the brush and proceed to the next section until the hair in the first section cools: Impatience means failure. Want more volume? Twist the hair on the brush in the opposite direction from the way you wish it to fall. Then brush and dry in the desired direction.

When hair is all dry from either method, bend over with your head down and brush and blow-dry from the roots to the tips for even greater volume—don't worry, you won't lose the curl or straightened effect. Then style.

Style It!

If you want to curl your hair
- Brush a styling product like mousse or gel through your wet hair.
- Divide the hair into small sections and hold with small clips.
- One by one, wrap each section around the bristles of a *narrow*, round brush and blow-dry.
- Allow each section to cool before you unroll the brush to go on to the next section.
- Roll the hair under to create a pageboy style.
- Roll it up and over the brush to give you a flip.

If you want to straighten your hair
- Use fat, round brushes.
- Gently pull each section of hair taut away from the roots as you dry around the fat brush.
- Release when cool.
- When hair is totally dry, use a flat paddle brush to further straighten, again using the dryer on medium heat on one section at a time. Start at the nape of the neck and brush underneath the hair from root to tip first. Brush over the surface for a straight, smooth finish.

HAIR CARE DOS AND DON'TS

DOS

- *Condition after a perm.* After a permanent, condition your hair each time you wash it, using conditioner diluted to half strength. Hair is porous after a chemical treatment. The opened hair shaft absorbs more conditioner than usual and full-strength conditioner tends to make hair lie flat and limp.

- *Take advantage of the steam room.* Steam baths or saunas will not damage your hair, despite rumors to the contrary. In fact, the steam room is a good place to condition with a protein conditioner after shampooing. Steam opens hair shafts and the conditioner penetrates more deeply.
- *Use fingertips, never nails, to work shampoo onto the scalp and through the hair.* If you like the feeling of nails, try a professional massage hairbrush to work the shampoo through. It's gentler than fingernails.
- *Buy small amounts of new products.* Purchase only the smallest travel-size bottle of a new product you're just going to try. Why be stuck with the jumbo economy size of a product you may hate?
- *Prevent split ends.* Applying a leave-in conditoner *only* to the very ends of your hair before using hot rollers or a curling iron.
- *Try vitamin E as a conditioner.* With a piece of cotton, spot the contents of one 400-unit capsule of vitamin E mixed with two tablespoons of soybean oil on split ends or other damaged areas of the hair. Comb through. Sit under a warm, wet towel for twenty minutes, then shampoo out. Apply the shampoo *before* you wet your hair—remember, oil and water don't mix! Finally, work into a lather and rinse thoroughly. By the way, a bit of vitamin E on a Q-Tip applied to a wound aids the healing.

DON'TS

- *Don't brush the proverbial hundred brushes a night.* The practice probably breaks and damages hair more than it gives shine and health. Your grandma told you to do it because in her day, women brushed so much in order to *clean* their hair. They believed a daily shampoo would make their hair fall out. Instead of brushing, try a nightly scalp massage with your fingers. It will do wonders to stimulate circulation in the head, which in turn is great for hair.
- *Don't overuse heavy, commercial conditioners.* They do make dry, brittle hair more supple, but if used too frequently they can leave a noticeable shine-reducing residue. For a change, try a natural product, like mayonnaise. Rub a *small* dab between your hands and apply it to just-washed hair; it coats, softens, and protects, and if you're blond, the lemon juice in the mayonnaise zips up the color.

Rinse with lukewarm water so your hair doesn't smell like salad dressing.

- *Don't have perms—even root perms—on the same day you color your hair.* Perms and coloring involve different sets of chemicals that, together, may damage the hair. And try not to have a full perm more than once a year. If your hair is shaped three to four times a year, you may have three or four gentle body waves.
- *Don't look for the shampoo with the most suds.* Suds add little to cleaning power and are difficult to rinse out.
- *Don't leave the salon without tips on how to maintain the brand-new cut or color.* A really good stylist will show you how to blow-dry the new cut, even if you don't spring for the cost of a blow-dry. You're a walking billboard for her, after all.

Five High-Tech Hair Tools

My clients with The Look can't live without certain hair tools, as integral to achieving The Look for hair as water is to healthy skin. Your beauty salon, hair-products specialty store, or even a drugstore may carry many of these products.

The perfect brushes. First of all, consider the metal-bodied round brush. Several manufacturers put them out now, but I like the Scalpmaster 5102 or the volumizing brush from Paul Mitchell. They hold the heat amazingly well when you style—far better than a brush with a plastic or wood structure, or even a curling iron. Also, I can't do without the Mason Pearson Popular Hairbrush, which now comes in pocket sizes. These rubber suction brushes don't pull the hair or create electricity. For knot removal, the Paul Mitchell Superbrush 427 is terrific. For styling long hair, you must have a large, three-inch-boar-bristle brush. Finally, the Aveda Paddle Brush straightens and lends gloss and polish.

Steam setters. Big hair is nicely achieved with heated rollers that use moisturizing-conditioning steam heat.

Velcro rollers. After a blow-dry, they give far greater lift and height than traditional rollers because they tug right into the hair. Velcro rollers come in an electric version, which makes for excellent lift and volume.

The super-powerful hair dryer. Hair dryers have been around forever, but none is as effective and powerful as Supersolano's 1600 red and black model. It comes with a handy cool-the-air-down button, which sets the hair (to order, call 800-323-3942).

It's not your mother's curling iron. There are many good curling irons to choose from, but big, fat supercurls can be had from a powerful, new curling iron that clients love, the Gold 'N Hot (available from Belson, call 818-763-7072) for its intense heat and polishing effect.

Five Old-fashioned Hair Tools

- *Long- or short-tooth grip combs*—a spring model that opens and snaps shut. These are can't-do-withouts for instant but stylish pull-backs or up-dos: I like them in tortoiseshell or clear plastic, and you can find them in any beauty supply store.
- *The lift pick.* A comb with a long, double-pronged end: You insert the pick into the hair where you need more volume, lift, and then spray-mist hair lightly. Remove the lift pick. Voilà! Height and volume.
- *The vintage narrow-tooth, tail comb.* There's nothing like it for teasing hair. You remember teasing: Back-comb two-inch sections at a time in a gentle stroke toward the roots; then smooth out on top with a what kind paddle brush.
- *The cowlick tamer—Scotch tape.* Tape across wet bangs or errant cowlicks until they dry. Nothing else works quite like it.
- *A box for your collection of hair stuff.* All the practical, everyday stuff that ends up in a million different hiding places when you're in a hurry ought to be consolidated. This includes plastic-tipped hairpins and bobby pins for chignons and French rolls and an assortment of barrettes, headbands, and cloth-covered elastic bands. One client keeps all her stuff in a wonderful Moroccan silver box on her dresser so that she can instantly find what she needs.

Hair jewelry—
a tortoiseshell cup.

BALANCE THE EQUATION

I've said that my favorite equation is ***Style = Texture × Cut, Color, and Care.*** Actually, there's one more style ingredient to consider. It's balance. Hairstyle must complement and balance your body's proportions. A tiny, short you will be dwarfed by big hair. A beautiful but heavy-set you will be rendered into pure bulk by big, curly hair—and look silly in too-small hair. You need a delicate balance. Our new equation:

Style = Texture × Cut, Color, and Care—and Balance

THE KEY TO THE CITY: A ROLE MODEL

Okay, so you have texture, cut, color, and care down pat. Now let's focus on style.

When it comes to a beautiful hairstyle, you can hold the key to the Big City Look in which you feel most comfortable by finding models to copy. "Copy" is not a bad word. Being a copycat is the simplest way, actually, to educate your taste. You experiment with hair and fashion possibilities by copying a woman who seems to have that marvelous look. Then perhaps you copy another. Before you know it, you'll be able to spot your true style, your personal best, the Big City Look most right for you. And others will be copying you!

Study your friends and the photographs of famous people whose hairstyle you'd want to emulate. Which person seems to have your face shape and similar hair texture? Be expansive, be daring, try not to choose a person who echoes only familiar beauty patterns. It takes a while to find an appropriate role model, but when you do, don't be shy. Examine her hair closely. Discuss or show her picture to your salon stylist to get an expert opinion. By the way, hairstylists don't yell anymore if you bring them pictures. Say you want to be a blonde—there are a thousand shades of blond. Bringing a photograph of the color you like will help me produce it.

If your stylist thinks the style you select is suitable for you, go further. Try to *literally* step into your role model's shoes, try to think about hair and clothes as she does. *Be that person* in your head for a little while. It works—believe me. One of my clients recounted the following story about choosing a hair *and* a fashion role model:

"Last week," said my client as she sat in the salon chair, "after I mentioned how fabulous I thought Katie's hair always looked—you told me you could see her look on me, and then you cut my hair in that same smart little-boy shag. When I left the salon I started to browse in Saks. I actually commanded my mind to think like Katie, choose like Katie. I felt pretty and really up for shopping with the new shag cut. And then the strangest thing happened: I was drawn to this little tan wool sheath that was unlike anything I'd ever worn before—but it looked just like Katie. One part of me said no; the other part said *try*! When I had it on, it looked like me.

"Well, guess what, Vincent?" said my client with a grin, "At the party that night, not only did Katie have my hair, but she was wearing the

same dress I'd selected. The *exact* dress. Now what are the odds of that happening? We laughed so hard when I told her the story. Frankly, I think the dress looked better on me. Also the hair."

What happened here? Clearly, Katie had the Big City Look, and my admiring client understood it would work for her as well. After a while, she no longer had to "think Katie." She learned how to do it herself.

Find a great role model, someone whose hair you love. Here are some photographs to help you—women with marvelous hair especially appropriate for specific regions of the country. These women hold the key to the Big City Look when it comes to hair. Do you think you want to emulate any? Do you and your hairstylist agree that you share similar face shapes and hair textures? Take this book to your stylist—and point.

Nina Griscom, cohost of the Food Network's *Dining Around* and wife of the preeminent plastic surgeon Dr. Daniel Baker, is the embodiment of the Big City Look in her tan cashmere turtleneck pullover by Michael Kors. Could you see her in New York? In L.A.? In Washington, D.C.? In Dallas? Chicago? Atlanta? I could. She has that universal Big City Look.

Emmy-winning broadcaster and two-time Olympic medalist swimmer Donna de Varona's hair has the perfect Chicago Big City Look. It's a graduated, soft-ends shag with chunks within the hair cut shorter to give a rippled effect when the wind blows. The cut gives great body and is extremely versatile, lending itself to different styles for a more formal look.

The Key to the Chicago Big City Hair Look? Real, Easy-Care, Wind-Proof Chic

WHO'S GOT IT? DONNA DE VARONA.
HOW'D SHE GET IT?

Donna's hair is a long, layered, moveable shag; it resists the wind because it loves the wind and blows with it—always returning to a soft, pretty effect. The cut is tapered close to the nape of the neck and the ends are not sharp but soft. The style is versatile: it can easily be transferred into a small French twist worn with or without bangs.

Blow-dry it to either side and use brushes of varying widths for volume. The fattest brush is best used on the outer, longer layers of hair and a medium-round brush smooths the shorter, underlayers and ends of the hair. Remember that the bigger the brush, the fuller the hair. If Donna wants more volume or curl—Velcro or hot rollers, strategically placed for just a few moments on the crown or underlayer of hair, do the trick.

L.A.'s honey-blond Morgan Fairchild (see p. 58) is quintessential West Coast. In a zippered pink satin shirt over a turtleneck, she's everyone's idea of Hollywood. Her hair is straight, long, blond, shiny, and very glamorous. (Photograph © Harry Langdon)

The Key to the L.A. Big City Hair Look? Glamour

WHO'S GOT IT? MORGAN FAIRCHILD. HOW'D SHE GET IT?

Morgan's hair is slightly layered around her face to frame it and around the halo of her head to achieve height: everywhere else it is all one length. Although she has a lot of hair, it is kept small and close to the head (not big and Texan at all). I think of it as sort of a modern, blond Cleopatra look even though it's not blunt-cut as Cleopatra's was. Her good, thick hair has a natural curl. For a supple smoothness and that California shine, I'd suggest using a gentle conditioner, but no mousse or gel in the styling. A few jumbo Velcro rollers placed high on the crown of the head provide height. A big, flat paddle brush gives great glisten and holds down the volume. As you blow-dry with the paddle brush, hold the hair smooth and taut, keeping the brush close to the scalp; follow along the tautly held hair from crown to tips of hair with the blow-dryer to attain a sleek, polished finish.

The Key to the D.C. Big City Hair Look? Understated, Flattering

WHO'S GOT IT? CLAIRE SHIPMAN, NBC CORRESPONDENT. HOW'D SHE GET IT?

Claire's hair is a clean-cut, serious, *un*geometeric, short, feather cut featuring light bangs and a clean neckline. It's best cut in many long layers above the ear, and the cut should not require brushes or rollers in the drying process. Using only the fingers as a comb, Claire's fine hair is air-blown *without* using a nozzle on the dryer. (The nozzle provides a more concentrated stream of air and less volume.) Blow the hair in the direction in which you want the hair to fall and aim the dryer directly at the roots to get the most volume.

The Key to the New York *Big City* Look? Short, Chic, Stunning, Often Experimental

WHO'S GOT IT? ROSE MARIE BRAVO. HOW'D SHE GET IT?

Rose Marie's hair is coarse and curly. She wears it small and close-cropped to the head—almost a little-boy look—in lots of short layers, cut clean over the ears and at the nape of the neck. On the crown of her head, the layers

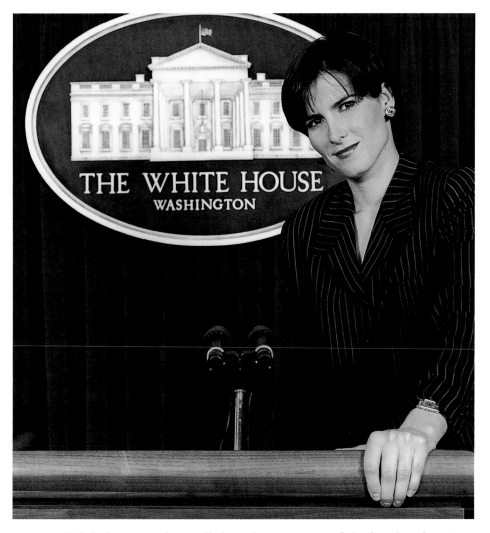

NBC correspondent Claire Shipman typifies the sleek, no-nonsense Washington, D.C., look. Understated in her navy pinstripe power suit, she's chic and ready for business. And that no-nonsense hair? At night she can gel it back for glamorous effect.

are cut slightly longer to keep all the volume on top of the head and to give off an air of unmistakeable femininity—belying the little boy in the style. The cut is blow-dried using small, round brushes (coarse, curly hair shouldn't be finger-dried). It's a good idea to apply lamination drops—available in beauty supply stores—while the hair is wet to seal the cuticle of the hair and calm the frizz. Using only about the size of a quarter's worth, mush the drops around in your hands, then through the scalp to the ends of the hair, fingers acting as a comb. You can even apply a smaller quantity of the lamination drops to the hair after it's dry. Wrap the hair around a small round brush. Then, using a dryer with a nozzle, aim a concentrated, steady stream of heat toward the roots of the hair, keeping the dryer at least six inches from the scalp. The result should be smooth and stunning.

Rose Marie Bravo, CEO of Burberry's, looking very New York in her Jil Sanders coat, Yves St. Laurent Rive Gauche skirt, and Yves St. Laurent turtleneck. Her hair is short, edgy, perfectly eclectic.

The Key to the Atlanta *Big City* Look?
Casual, Pretty, Watch for the Hairbands!

WHO'S GOT IT? NICOLE MASERANTONIO.
HOW'D SHE GET IT?

Nicole has a shining, smooth bob with bangs and lots of highlights added to the color. In fact, nothing in the hair is layered except those thick, chunky bangs; one top layer is left slightly longer so that it locks under the rest of the hair to give it an angled look. The hair is cut shorter at the nape of the neck and the look is neat and controlled—per Atlanta standards. Use a round, fat brush without a nozzle as you blow dry the sides and front, a smaller round brush to blow-dry the hair at the nape of the neck, and a medium round brush for the crown. A nozzle on the blow-dryer then directs the air to that longer outer layer held taut with a brush for the smooth Atlanta look.

If you like a headband, pull it over your head first as if it was a necklace, then pull it up behind the ears. This gives height to the back and crown. After the band is placed, you can, if you wish, pull out a few tendrils for a whimsical, softer look.

Nicole has it—that Atlanta Big City Look. Perfectly blond, bobbed, head-banded, and gracious.

The Key to the Dallas *Big City* Hair Look?
Wonderful, Wild Big Hair

WHO'S GOT IT? ROSIE MONCRIEF.
HOW'D SHE GET IT?

Big hair has gotten a bad rap from the media, but done right—as seen in the photograph of Dallas-Fort Worth's Rosie Moncrief—it's one of the sexiest, prettiest, freshest looks around. Pancake hair, flat to the head is definitely not this Big City Look. There are more waves, more bangs, more curl, more volume—more of everything going on with Texas hair.

The hair is cut in long layers, keeping all the volume at the sides and nape of the neck. Often the ends of the hair are layered (not cut blunt) for a classic Texas flip.

A Dallas-Fort Worth woman washes her hair often because she knows natural oils weigh it down and flatten it. She usually applies a gentle amount of volumizing spray or mousse or gel to the roots that she lifts away from the scalp as she blow-dries with a fat, round brush. She flips and dries her hair to the left and then to the right and repeats the entire process several times. For really big hair, she sections off her hair, placing a fat, supergrip Velcro roller in each section for just a few moments. Then she blow-dries, section by section, using a diffuser attachment on a dryer set to medium-hot and high speed; finally, she switches to cool to really *set* the curls.

After the hair is dry, she bends her head down, brushes in an up direction, straightens her neck, then styles and smooths. Voilà—BIG hair.

STREET SMARTS

One of the most endearing qualities about the woman with the Big City Look is her street smarts—and that goes for hair as well as being savvy in self-defense. She knows how to deal with muggers *and* she knows how to deal with bad-hair days—almost as scary. She has cutting-edge products perfect for her needs, as well as the golden-oldie hair tools. She doesn't get thrown by special needs for special occasions. Here are only some of her street smarts.

Ayurveda

What if you've got all your hair, but it looks washed out and tired? Want a breath of fresh hair? Try an ayurvedic rinse and shampoo. The

newest and also age-old street savvy popularized by health and beauty gurus like Deepak Chopra and the Indian beauty expert Pratima Raichur raises hair care to a new art form. The emphasis is on the ancient and natural Hindu healing art called ayurveda—literally, the science of living to a ripe old age. Ayurvedic practice involves the use of herbal powders, essences, and oils in hair and skin care and also stresses the importance of daily scalp massages to stimulate oxygen and blood flow. Some natural ayurvedic concoctions to try on your own hair:

- Vinegar used diluted as a rinse. It gets rid of soap, cuts the oil in blond hair, and makes the color brighter. If you like, you can follow with a conditioner.

Businesswoman Rosie Moncrief, the quintessential yellow rose of Texas. Her hair is wild and wonderful and very, very Texas. (Photograph © James Richter)

Some perfect tools: rollers in many sizes. The paddle brush. The metal-bodied round brush. The grip comb in pretty tortoiseshell. A tortoiseshell cup for catching the hair in a chignon. Two hair extensions—match the braided piece to your hair at the base of your neck and voilà—a whole new style. Or wrap the longer hair extension (in a color that matches yours) around the base of the ponytail. A cloth-covered elastic band adorned with a small bow changes a plain ponytail into city style.

- Beer, mashed avocado, and egg can all give fullness. Rinse them out after applying unless you want *very* sticky hair.
- Lemon juice can be marvelous for blondes if your hair is not too dry—the acid in lemons can be drying. Dilute the juice of one lemon with water and massage through the hair. Rinse well and condition, if you like.
- My favorite? Rainwater. If you don't mind collecting this precious essence, it's marvelous for rinsing all textures and shades of hair.

Ayurveda forbids the use of chemical coloring agents, metal brushes, and permanent waves. I *love* the proper use of chemical coloring agents, metal brushes, and permanent waves—the best science has to offer. So what's a woman to do? Moderation in all techniques is, for me, the truest route to beauty. It's been my experience that a reasonable combination of approaches works best.

Hair Today, Gone Tomorrow

No chapter on hair would be complete without offering some street savvy on a problem that is not only your uncle's. More women than you'd guess have hair loss, and, as with even more personal matters, only their

hairdressers know because they have taught them how to disguise the evidence. Not that baldness automatically takes one out of the Big City Look category. Ever see the photographs of a totally bald Elizabeth Taylor after her brain surgery? Her *attitude* made The Look. With or without hair, she's fantastic. Ditto one of the most charismatic and exquisite women I know, Princess Caroline of Monaco. When the press exploited her temporary hair loss, she achieved The Look as beautifully with the turbans she wore and the panache with which she wrapped them around her head as when we saw her with a stylish hairdo.

Still, I don't mean to propose flaunting baldness as a way to go. If you have thinning hair, there are many ways to deal with it.

WHAT CAUSES THE PROBLEM?

Sometimes the cause is genetic (androgenetic alopecia, or female-pattern baldness), which is characterized by the hair's thinning evenly across the scalp. Sometimes skin disease is the underlying culprit, in which case generally round, clearly defined patches of baldness are seen. Skin disorders like psoriasis, infectious diseases like ringworm, or, more rarely, even adrenal or thyroid tumors can be at fault. As soon as you spot thinning patches, consult a physician, starting with a dermatologist.

Medication can certainly cause hair loss. Chemotherapy is the most widely recognized culprit, and recipients may lose almost all their hair, but it does grow back when chemo is discontinued. Other medications like blood thinners, antibiotics, and cholesterol-reducing agents can produce less dramatic hair loss. Losing one's hair after giving birth is quite common: It is caused by a sharp drop in a woman's estrogen level. Finally, damage to hair roots from improper hair care like too much teasing or pulling, constant dieting, and/or nutritional deficiencies can also produce hair loss.

WHAT TO DO?

In most circumstances, most of the time, normal hair growth returns all by itself. When it doesn't, medications like over-the-counter Rogaine, used to treat hereditary hair loss, can be tried. Hair transplant surgery is always an option, as are artificial hairpieces, cleverly inserted.

From my point of view, the best results to deal with thinning hair are obtained by a marvelous cut, careful camouflage in styling techniques, and judicious hair care. Total hair coloring or even gentle highlights add a real sense of volume. An excellent hairdresser can—with bangs, body waves, and other styling techniques—make hair-thickening magic. Teasing or back-combing also makes hair look thicker and hides bald patches, but gently, please, and with a wide-toothed plastic comb.

CAUTIONS

- Excessive bleaching and harsh permanent waving can cause temporary hair loss; make sure your hairstylist is a pro.
- Very hot hair dryers are not terrific for any hair and are disastrous for thinning hair. After shampooing, brush *very* lightly with a soft brush, and make sure your hair is totally dry before you brush more briskly.
- Forget about the one hundred nightly brushes your mother advised. That's not good for anyone—especially you.
- Hold the hair dryer at least eight inches from your head.
- Tight pulling of the hair (into a ponytail or onto rollers) often causes hair loss to develop. Do not use any hairstyle that depends on heavy tension. That means no uncovered rubber bands. Ever.
- Heavy hair spray will clump thin hair and make it look even thinner. Light hair spray is your friend: Spray on the roots—where volume comes from—for fuller-looking hair.

Tips for Special Occasions: Ask Vincent

I'm planning my wedding and I think I want my hair to be curly—and maybe even blonder—on that special day. When should I do all this?

Experiment with color or perming at least four to eight weeks before the wedding—not the week before—to make sure you have time to fix any potential disasters. Also make sure your stylist tries your chosen hairstyle with your bridal headpiece at least once before the big day.

I've got a last-minute business presentation that's very important to me. How can I get some instant body into this limp hair?

A little gel rubbed between your hands and "combed" into the hair gives a wet look even as it provides some structure. Don't use too much because it will weigh the hair down, making it even limper. Also try turning your head upside down and spraying into the roots, then styling.

I plan to do some television work and I want some highlights put into my dark hair. Any tips?

Avoid red. Television lights intensify red tones and make them look garish. Ask your stylist to try soft caramel or rich auburn lights at least two weeks before the big day.

I'm taking out some very important clients on Christmas Eve. How do I achieve a serious, chic, and different look with my long hair—without a trip to the hairdresser?

How about a double ponytail?

Pull your hair back from your face and divide it into two sections with a part running around the back of your head from ear to ear. One section will include the hair at the top of the head; the other, all the hair underneath. Secure each section with a covered elastic. Tuck each section of hair under itself. Secure both with bobby pins. The result resembles a double chignon. Finish off with pretty hair jewelry at the base of the double tail.

I have a big party on Sunday and I'm planning to stay up all Saturday night because sleeping is murder on my hair. The morning after I have my

hair done, I invariably wake up with a head full of knots, tangles, and hair going in all different directions. How do I preserve Saturday's salon-perfect hair—and still catch a few winks?

I hear about this problem from more people than you'd dream. Solution? A satin pillow.

I'm meeting the mother of the man of my dreams in an hour and I'm having a bad-hair day. It's my worst nightmare.

You can wake up from the nightmare now. Even street-smart women suffer bad-hair days, but they know how to disguise the disasters. They've learned from the street by watching savvy teenagers as well as high-fashion models with The Look. For starters, try stunning, oversize shades pushed back on your head to contain hair frizzies. Jacqueline Onassis always wore sunglasses to control her hair on a bad-hair day and look chic at the same time. Ponytails and up-dos can also disguise the havoc of a humid afternoon. They look fine with hair jewelry like jeweled bobby pins, barrettes, marvelous headbands, or tortoiseshell grip combs. Beautiful scarves can also cover a multitude of evils. Finally, when all else fails, rely on a stunning hat or cap. It may look so chic, you'll never leave home without it.

I'm going to a costume party and I want to temporarily change the color of my hair. What do you think?

Hair jewelry: grip combs, ponytail holders, and tortoiseshell cups are fine hair accessories. They change a look immediately.

For a bad hair day . . . try a scarf.

Don't do it. Sure, you can use a temporary rinse or hair-color spray, but personally, I'd never advise putting cheap chemicals (and that's what these products are made of) on one's hair. At all costs, avoid any product made to last through more than one shampoo. Wear a wig.

My hair looks okay for New Year's Eve, but I have a tough time with makeup. I need some expert advice and I can't afford an expert.
At lunchtime, go to the best department store in your city and ask for a makeover at your favorite makeup counter. You're doing *them* a service—people love to watch, then buy what looked good on you. And don't feel obliged to buy products you don't love, even if you've gotten a great makeover.

THE LAST WORD ON HAIR

Hair identifies us more than anything else—more than skin, perfect features, clothes. Visualize the most interesting-looking celebrities you know of. Think Diane Sawyer, Liza Minnelli, Veronica Lake, Marilyn Monroe, Whoopi Goldberg, Courteney Cox, Katie Couric, Julia Louis-Dreyfus. Would you describe them by their clothes, eyes, skin color—or hair? I choose their fabulous hair.

Which description would *you* choose?
- *The blond bombshell* or *the woman with great skin*
- *The raven-haired beauty* or *the well-dressed beauty*
- *The strawberry blonde* or *the woman with good posture*

The hair wins, every time.

Especially if it's got that Big City Look.

CHAPTER TWO
FASHION

CRYSTAL-BALL TIME

Do you want me to tell you about a fashion designer who struck out in the crystal-ball department? Years ago, a Vienna-born fashion guru was asked to predict the fashion of the future. He described a time when women would no longer consider romance in their clothes. He said that tomorrow's woman would get rid of her jewelry and cosmetics and dress like tomorrow's man. The aesthetics of fashion, he said, would involve training the body to grow beautifully—rather than covering it up to produce beauty. As for old people, he predicted that they'd adopt a uniform of their own.

Bad predicting. Fashion and style will always count wherever women love surprise and romance and feeling good about themselves as women, not as imitators of men.

Try telling the zillion-dollar fashion industry that romance is dead and the American woman won't be buying

And at night when the stars come out . . . Fabulous Natalie Cole in her glorious beaded pantsuit on the staircase of her home. Pure L.A. glamour. Her daddy would be proud. Wardrobe by Cecille Parker.

clothes this year because she's investing all her time and money in making only her body beautiful. Try telling your gorgeous seventy-year-old aunt Florence that she will have to adopt a uniform of the aged instead of looking ageless, looking like a million.

The dubious fashion guru was Rudi Gernreich; the year he said all this would happen was 2000. He was wronger than wrong.

Chic . . . and Shock

More prescient was the late Italian designer Gianni Versace. In a *New York Times* interview just before he died, he predicted that the interesting use of fashion would always be an important component of extraordinary women.

The American women whose fashion most inspired Versace, he said, had both *chic* and *shock*. Think about that: chic . . . and shock! What a memorable combination! Although Versace was thinking specifically of Madonna and Courtney Love, there's no doubt in my mind that he was also talking about the American woman with the Big City Look. Wherever she lives—in Dallas, in Washington, in Atlanta—she certainly offers the most delightful wit, chic, and shocks in her clothes, in her style.

The old-time loyalty to one designer has gone out the window. Instead, experimentation is the current mind-set. "Everyone else's fashion is the true American fashion," said Versace. It's true—and that's why I admired him. He saw that American women *are* of the world. They adopt and adapt what they need—and have no qualms about mixing and matching. They incorporate a sense of chic with the shock of big city. Christian Lacroix, the noted French designer, said that the quintessential American clothing item was jeans and that athletic-wear clothing was "the true American fashion." Also true. Yohji Yamamoto, the extraordinary Japanese designer, said that authentic American style was "hip-hop, black rap musicians' loose and baggy pants." Also true.

How Can It All Be True?

It can. The woman with the Big City Look has universal style. And style is a dizzying, glamorous aura that has less to do with the choice of a particular dress or the color of a purse than with the total *effect*—the way some women know how to put themselves together to make an impression. Women with the Big City Look reimagine themselves often, then reinvent

True American fashion: well-cut, simple jeans as worn by Silke.

themselves with elegant, attention-demanding fashion. What an enchanting tool—reinvention. You rarely bore anyone when you're capable of seeing yourself in a new way.

Geography and Fashion

Finally I come to the noted American designer Bill Blass. Blass, perhaps better than any of the others, understands American fashion as exemplified by the Big City Look.

"How people dress has so much to do with geography," says Blass. "There is a California style, a Texas style, a San Francisco style, a New York style. It has to do with the sky. With a way of life."

Most true of all.

The woman with The Look thrives on wearing fashion that pleases her, fashion that's appropriate for the region from which she hails, and fashion that is both chic . . . and shock. But mostly chic.

What does she look like, this unforgettable woman?

THE CITY CODES: FASHION
Cracking the Western Code:
The Look of Los Angeles Fashion

Remember the L.A. Code Word: Glamour. Los Angeles is a fantasy town—flashdance leggings, glittery see-through chemises, easy slip-dresses, spike heels for evening, and those Levi's everywhere. Watch for diamond stud earrings and Rolex watches on the tennis court, and never forget the neat little Louis Vuitton sack to carry your tennis racquet.

The only fashion rule in L.A. is: *Wear what's right for you and put your own stamp on it!* All other fashion rules will inevitably be broken.

The secret to style in this town is often in the unexpected—a hint of outrageous color, a mix of fabrics you probably wouldn't wear to the office in Chicago. Heavy hitters in the City of the Angels are also clothes that reflect L.A.'s whimsical energy: Winnie the Pooh backpacks, white duck pants headed for the Studio City Golf Course, and, if you're young and slim and outrageous enough, lingerie worn on the outside (probably from the local boutique Trashy Lingerie).

L.A. women reflect that Southern California "nobody-was-actually-born-here" sensibility. Still, they all seem to be connected to Hollywood,

they all love gossamer-light short-skirted knits to take them to work, and, afterward, on the pub crawl with pals, and they all wear T-shirts, tennis skirts, and Nikes or loafers on weekend afternoons. And at night, when the stars come out for the openings and the benefits and the screenings and the Beverly Hills dinner parties? Look for scandalously sheer shirts mixed with very sharp tailoring, relaxed glamour, and always, that personal, individualistic style. L.A. women don't really give a hoot whether the "little nothing" slip-dress is a fashion trend or not. They make their own fashion. The city is nothing if not daring.

The neighborhood shopping watch here takes us to neighborhoods like Los Feliz, the SoHo of L.A., which sport boutiques like X-Girl, which sells silk print pants and dark denims, and SquaresVille, which sells vintage Gucci, Hermès, and Dior. A great shopping street? La Brea, between

What shines through the Big City Look? Sure—beauty, fashion, and attitude are integral parts—but there's also courage and talent. Sometimes all these attributes come in a single package: Vanessa Williams. (Photograph © Sante D'Orazio)

L.A. by day: The low-rise jeans, the tank top, the shades. The Big City Look in L.A. is funky, casual, glamorous. L.A. by night: The exquisite, gossamer-sheer slip gown goes to the Awards or maybe even just to your house for dinner. L.A. can carry off anything.

Wilshire and Sunset.

Even people who swear they don't shop cruise the racks at the Ron Herman/Fred Segal specialty store on Melrose. John Eshayua, style guru, fashion barometer, and vice president of Herman/Segal on Melrose, says that ethnic looks along with halters, vintage anything, sexy heels, and shower sandals are typical of the L.A. look. The woman with the Big City Look may decide to scratch the shower sandals. *I'd* advise that, anyway.

If there's one problem in L.A., it's a kind of fashion schizophrenia that the woman with the Big City Look will instinctively avoid. "The biggest fashion mistake I see," says Eshayua, "is too many trends at once—like a twin sweater set, rubber sandals, a backpack, and low-rise jeans, and a belly-button ring showing."

L.A. STREET SIGNS

- Miniskirts for everyone under forty and long skirts with very high slits for everyone.
- Great pedicures.
- Cappuccino in one hand, with Rollerblades on the feet.
- The tucked-in-at-one-hip sweater (worn with a hip-slung skirt).
- Fanatics looking for bargains at the Rose Bowl Flea Market (second Sunday of the month in Pasadena).
- Tank tops; L.A. thrives on tanks.
- Levi's 501's.
- The cross-shopping young, sporting Prada or Gucci bags with jeans and a T-shirt from Guess?

Cracking the Midwest Code: The Look of Chicago Fashion

Remember the Chicago Code Word: Real. Everything about the city of Chicago feels rough and tough—after all, it's the "city of the big shoulders." Even the thrusting architecture, including the Sears Tower—the world's tallest building—shouts *masculine*. Forget nostalgia, romantic, tradition—this is a city that looks forward and likes comfort.

Chicago women are not masculine by any stretch of the imagination, but they are lovely and down-to-earth. They always know how the game went and drop team names at cocktail parties—"Go *Bears*!" They want clothes to *work* against the punishing cold. They may not buy a new evening outfit every year, but you can bet your bottom dollar they buy a new winter coat every year. Shearling coats sell out by August, says one Chicago fashion buyer.

"'Exciting but practical' is the ethic here—and 'I don't want to spend my whole day shopping,'" says Phyllis Schwartz, a longtime Chicago resident transplanted from New York.

"I don't like to look crazy," says a Chicago stock analyst, "so I won't buy whatever designers dish up. I think most women know what they want. Smart designers listen. Give me the old cashmere sweater sets any day and a pretty but warm wrap for over my dress-up clothes."

Joan Weinstein, the president of the upscale store Ultimo in Chicago, says, "We certainly do find the juxtaposition of masculine/feminine most interesting, as in the Gucci strong-shouldered easy jacket and the sexy side-slit knee skirt; as in the strict leather for day and the dramatic, glamorous dresses for evening . . . a return to womanliness, but more man-meets-woman than boy-meets-girl."

"There's a whole lot of slacks going on," says another chic Chicagoan.

Clearly, there's a whole lot of individual taste going on. Chicago women adore Calvin Klein. The smooth, honest appeal of Richard Tyler, Donna Karan, and Ralph Lauren always find a warm spot in the heart of the Windy City woman. Chicago women try something new at least once a year—always within reason and always in good taste.

About shoes: This is a true urban environment where it's often easier to walk than to drive—so forget stilettos, even if it's a stiletto-trend year.

Chicagoans hate underwear as outerwear, for example, satin brassieres under designer evening jackets or even the omnipresent (everywhere else) slip-dresses. Pragmatic to the core, these women will not fall victim to designer silliness. They have lives.

Still, they love fashion. Charles Ifergan, the famed Chicago stylist, says, "Chicago used to be a hick town—my clients would go twice a year to New York to shop. No more. Now the media is the message, and hundreds of magazines, television, and the Internet have changed the attitude of Chicago to fashion. At night women play with sensuality, and although we're not talking showing up in your underwear, they still exhibit a lot more skin than they ever did before; there's a definite difference in attitude. While the New York woman says, 'I dare you to look at me,' the Chicagoan says, 'This is me. What you see is what you get.'"

Chicago by day: A fabulous, full greatcoat ending just below midcalf is perfect over slacks or a dress. Chicagoans love their coats cut well so they look wonderful when worn fully open.
Chicago by night: Georgeous, stylish—but don't forget the wrap.

Actress and director Joanna Kerns (*Growing Pains*) in a perfectly cut Richard Tyler white tuxedo pantsuit.

Kate Moore has the perfect Chicago Big City Look in her periwinkle-blue plaid Valentine jacket.

IN CHICAGO

- you can wear the same outfit twice.
- you don't have to be on the cutting edge. You can wear a Jil Sander hot off the runway to one charity event and an oldie but goodie (really old—you wore it in college) formal suit to the next do.
- no one is fooled by trends.
- no one wears black all the time—as she might in New York.
- you're in a one-piece-of-jewelry-at-a-time town—unlike, say, Dallas.
- instead of saying "Give me something backless," women are more likely to say "Give me something with sleeves."

CHICAGO STREET SIGNS

- Car coats, car coats, car coats.
- Weathered Ralph Lauren men's khakis and jeans—on women —and bootleg pants.
- Low-slung, knee-length skirts.
- Oprah Winfrey in her jogging togs with Solomon the cocker spaniel trotting alongside.
- Boots, boots, boots—ankle-length, calf-length, thigh-high.
- Hush Puppies.
- Black wool turtlenecks under tan cashmere polo coats.
- Leggings.
- Dresses with jackets.
- Politically incorrect or not—those furs. You'll definitely see them in Chicago, my dear, so brace yourself.
- Never a bare midriff—even in August.

Cracking the Mid-Atlantic Code: The Look of D.C. Fashion

Remember the Washington, D.C., Code Word: Understated. What's fashion for? The answer used to be to announce your wealth, but in Washington, D.C., most women use fashion to convey what they do. Here more than in any other city, clothes are public signals that communicate not only personal style but business ethics and values.

Washington women opt for fashion that makes them look as if they're in charge of their workday as well as their sexuality, femininity, and integrity.

Independent-minded designers reign here. D.C. women easily mix and match their fashions because they usually choose clothes that can be

Washington by day: The Big City Washington woman is stunning, understated, and all business in her well-fitting pinstripe suit, jewel-necked blouse, proper (but fabulous) pearls, spectator shoes, and envelope purse for her papers. She's in charge.

Washington at night: All stops are pulled for the inaugural, charity, or embassy balls. With her hair piled up, the layers and layers of extravaganza ball gown, and the long gloves reminiscent of another era, the D.C. woman's Big City Night look is dynamite.

A feather cut should work for its wearer in fast, easy, and pretty presentation. At night, NBC Washington correspondent Claire Shipman can gel her hair back and turn from talented professional into glamour girl.

worn from daytime into evening in good, high style and comfortable design.

"You can't go wrong with Donna Karan or Liz Claiborne" is the mantra of a Chevy Chase Circle stockbroker. "Skirt lengths are conservative but not dumpy, usually ending at or just above the knee. Add a low utilitarian heel—preferably a patent leather pump—and you look like you belong here." The most popular labels for women diplomats as well as diplomats' wives are Chanel and Valentino, while the Capitol crowd opts for Brooks Brothers and Britches. The most popular clothing colors for everyone are red or navy.

A government analyst, getting to the point of Washington fashion, says, "Suits? Yes—but Washington women know that suits don't have to be uniforms." She's right. Whether one opts for a big, boxy construction (*you try getting in and out of those commuter airplanes in a tight little number*), an androgynous pantsuit, or a tunic jacket with a sexy miniskirt, suits are de rigueur. Suits mean business, but they also must be good-looking. The loveliest come tailored in the most gossamer of wools, the most buttery leathers, or even a high-tech synthetic blend.

As in Chicago, the women here are *real*. The *Washington Post*'s fashion editor, Robin Givhan, says she loves the ethic of "the older Italian women, with their sense of themselves, their understanding that they get more interesting with time." Pitch them against the "runway wraiths" with their impractical fashions—and the real woman wins every time. Washington is nothing if not a serious town.

Givhan sums it up in an interview with *The Washingtonian:* Washington women, she says, are smart, sophisticated, and international, with wildly varying roots. So expect *everything.* For example, although the often wicked-looking Versace style is not terribly popular here, you'll always find one woman who will buy a Versace chain-mail evening dress. You'll note that the church-lady segment of the population feels best when wearing suits, hats, and shoes to match. The Capitol Hill women feel best in St. John's knit suits that say they're in control and don't want what they're wearing to distract from what they say. And, says the fashion editor, the young crowd dresses in somewhat different and eclectic ways in mildly unusual clothes, probably picked up at a store in Bethesda called Relish. Givhan, incidentally, hates women walking to work in sneakers because they don't appear serious enough, and she also hates white stockings—too nurselike.

In the end, every Washington woman wants the same thing: to feel stylish and comfortable and, most of all, appropriate.

WASHINGTON STREET SIGNS
- The pinstripe skirt suit.
- Power pantsuits in black, gray, or dark blue.
- Big, lush cashmere scarfs draped over a suited shoulder.
- The single strand of pearls.
- The cell phone (now in designer colors).
- Fur. With all due respect to animal rights groups, Washington, like Chicago, gets its minks out of storage every winter.

Finally, what's hip in Washington? Nothing.

Cracking the Eastern Code: The Look of New York Fashion

Remember the New York Code Word: Eclectic. Here, keeping the edge counts.

One year it's minimalism. The next, those same designers who eschewed the teeniest flounce will be dabbling in beads and color. One year, sensible square toes; next year, spike heels. The year after? Who knows?

You do know this: If it's New York, it's the newest fashion trends—before most of the rest of the world has even heard about them. The late designer Versace pointed out, "New York women are the first to follow the trends set all over the world. They take from the Japanese, from the French. They will wear tennis shoes with a Chanel jacket."

In New York, no one's afraid to be first in fashion, no one's afraid she's out of line because she's added an insane touch to her fashion palette. In New York, you *want* to be out of line, and everyone's a little insane. The eclectic look of New York includes every designer ever to give a trunk show in Saks, the artsy-craftsy vintage Village style, silk charmeuse T-shirts, and even the glitz of an occasional drag queen, not to mention the best street fashion, even more significant here than couture—and make no mistake, there's *plenty* of couture.

New York takes fashion risks: One even sees tantalizing touches—embroidery, beading, or tulle—usually reserved for nighttime discreetly showing up in the office, and they look absolutely appropriate! Accepted fashion codes such as "White in the summer only" are thrown out the window. Here, urban white is just as big in the winter—cool, powerful, and streamlined. *Glamour* magazine's Susie Yalof says it takes a certain type of person to break the accepted fashion code, but getting away with breaking fashion rules is all about confidence—the mark of the New York woman with the Big City Look. "Go ahead," says Yalof, "wear white pants in January. Just keep your nose in the air and you can do it!"

What does New York dressed down look like? Mostly androgynously stunning women, a genderless generation with a wardrobe that includes jeans—those Levi's 501's, cable-knit sweaters, and Timberland boots on men, women, children, and nannies. Even the homeless are occasionally spotted in those Timberlands. And shades, always shades. And sweaters knotted over the shoulder or around the hips. And pantsuits—the most smashingly tailored suits. And, of course, touches the rest of the world wouldn't be caught dead in added to a man-tailored jacket—perhaps a beaded T-shirt, perhaps no shirt at all. You're not in Kansas anymore, Dorothy.

New York dressed up? Almost anything goes. For a sparkling opera evening, one might see a woman in a drop-dead vintage Fortuny gown that she spotted at a favorite flea market for a fraction of what it would have cost even when you could buy a new Fortuny. Notice the vintage crystal beads. You might also spot the simplest of little black dresses—also the height of chic. You might also see a buttoned-down Issaye Miyake pleated

A sweater knotted over the shoulder is a typical New York touch.

column dress that takes your breath away. You might also see jeans—topped with a smashing jacket. Jeans at the opera? Yes. I saw them. And the wearer was stunning.

Women in New York absorb, then re-create for themselves, the fashion that they're exposed to by the department stores, magazines, and peddlers on the street. They do it through details—concrete details in the concrete city: It's these details that lend sidewalk savvy. For instance, a fabulous suit from Saks Fifth Avenue, a blouse from a Third Avenue street fair, a men's vest from The Gap, a wool cape from a thrift shop, a chenille scarf from a children's catalogue like Hanna Andersson, a silver pin from Rico the street peddler. The woman with The Look layers it and wears it—all at once.

Want to see the New York woman with the Big City Look? Keep your eyes open and stand quietly (pretend you're waiting for your lover)

- right in front of Saks Fifth Avenue, at Fiftieth and Fifth Avenue, across the street from St. Patrick's Cathedral. The woman could emerge from a limo, or from a nearby subway, so keep your eyes peeled in every direction. You'll know her when you see her.
- at the intersection of Fifty-ninth and Lexington, where The Gap, Banana Republic, and Bloomingdale's are all a charge card's throw from one another. You'll know her when you see her.
- smack in the middle of SoHo, where the boutiques, the neighborhood residents, the street vendors, and the passersby all vie for the title of "most interesting." You'll know her when you see her.

NEW YORK STREET SIGNS

- The water bottle.
- Black. Blacker than night, blacker than black is the strongest color in New York, day or night. It really is. Black *is* style here—so much so that plastic splints for broken wrists or arms are even popping up in black!
- A knock-off Prada purse or a handmade silver choker from a SoHo street peddler.
- A Walkman.
- Backpacks in every fabric, every configuration—except animals. Women with the New York look don't wear little stuffed bears on their backs.
- Vintage clothing and jewelry from the Sunday flea market at Twenty-sixth and Avenue of the Americas.

New York by day: A chic, well-fitting pantsuit, a purse with a scarf tied on for attitude, and bold gold earrings finish the look.

New York by night: On the edge! A black velvet sheath with ethnic bracelets worn high on the arm, fishnet stockings, and stilettos.

The Big City Look lives everywhere—even on the ice at New York's Rockefeller Center ice rink. Here's champion skater Jo Jo Starbuck, in a wonderful cable-knit sweater and tights, holding me up!

One of my all-time favorites, exquisite Julia Ormond wearing black, black, black—the chosen color for Big Apple fashion.

Atlanta by day: On a sunny Saturday afternoon, look for the Atlantan on the courts— cute, chic, and stylish. Check out the hairband—she has it in every fabric and color.

Atlanta by night: She's got big-city class in her elegant Chanel– or St. John–type suit. One piece of great heirloom jewelry and the ubiquitous hairband in her Atlanta bob and she's off to dinner at the club. She's a lady!

Cracking the Southern Code:
The Look of Atlanta Fashion

The Question: What's fashion for? The Answer: Southern Comfort (Remember Atlanta's Code Words).

In this part of the South, daytime fashion embraces ease, comfort, *pretty*, and the defining words are "Is it machine washable?"

The Atlanta woman often resembles a Ralph Lauren ad, a look that one Atlanta woman has characterized as "WASP-wear." We're talking Banana Republic, J. Crew, Calvin Klein, Ann Taylor, Talbot's, Martha Stewart—definitely *not* Prada's crimson chiffon mandarin jacket. Jay Reynolds, one of Atlanta's local designers, has been quoted as saying, "Atlanta style has gotten extremely simple. If I even put a bow on a dress, they shriek!" In Atlanta and in other parts of the South, somehow it's not so important for women to look hip. What is important is that they look classy.

Pared-down and body-conscious resort wear is most popular here—think cool ice-cream-colored linens and the ubiquitous white blazer with navy slacks—although most Atlanta women won't wear white after Labor Day, an old hard-and-fast rule. The delicate silks, the golf outfits, the dress-plus-jacket for those air-conditioned restaurants are also very Georgia.

Atlantans are stylish but they're not shopaholics. Most own many little "just-for-this-season" outfits but only one or two great keepers, says the Atlanta hairstylist Carey Carter. "We're big on shoes here—expensive, highly styled shoes. We're not so big on jewelry—a little bit of the real stuff goes a long way." One Atlantan, resplendent in her gold hoop earrings, says, "We *sleep* in our earrings!"

The Georgia woman with The Look demands great design, no matter how heavy she is. Bodies of all shapes and sizes look neat and pretty here, never sloppy. To that end, the Atlanta woman often turns to local designers who will allow her to have a say in fabric, cut, color, and shape. For example, here are five of Atlanta's growing group of high-style designers:

- Jay Reynolds—Evening and special-occasion gowns.
- Wayne Van Nugyen—"Cool, funky" are his code words.
- Edgar Pomeroy—Well-cut suits in fine fabrics.
- Knox Clayton—Classic, sophisticated clothing is his mantra.
- Marcia Sherrill—Fine jewelry and leather accessories.

Atlanta is a city of old-time nostalgia. With Atlanta's famous leafy trees sheltering many metro neighborhoods, nearly everyone has, at the very least, a shady corner with a hammock . . . and nearly everyone has dumped the Scarlett O'Hara wasp-waist mentality for easygoing clothes and a swell mint julep.

"Vulgar" is the word Atlantans use for what they hate:

- Black stockings with white patent stilettos? *Vulgar.*
- White to a wedding unless you're the bride? *Vulgar.*
- Black after Memorial Day? *Vulgar.*
- Pants in the evening, even *evening* pants? *Vulgar.*
- Calf-length skirts? *Vulgar.*

ATLANTA STREET SIGNS

- Headbands; white visors.
- Tennis togs—very stylish tennis togs. Also very short.
- Vintage gold circle pins—Atlantans love to wear a family jewelry heirloom with a pared-down, ultramodern outfit.
- Debutante dresses, from plain to froufrou—always in white or pastel shades.
- Pretty women in flowered skirts and body-skimming dresses at arts festivals.
- Very well dressed supermarket shoppers. In Atlanta, women won't go to the supermarket without styling their hair, putting on fresh makeup, and dressing up.

Cracking the Southwest Code: The Look of Dallas Fashion

Remember the Dallas Code Word: Rich. "Who's to say what's excessive?" asks one Dallas beauty. "Criticize our dressing up all you like, but if you're going to be the fashion police, stay in your neat little conservative box all by yourself. The rest of us are going shopping."

That pretty much sums up the Dallas attitude, which is . . . Shop till you drop. We all need something great to wear to the Cattle Barons' Ball. Fashion in Dallas usually turns out to be pure, glamorous high style—lots of Armani and Jil Sander, lots of tulle, lots of leather, lots of jewelry, lots of white tie. In Dallas, men often don a pair of cowboy boots with an Armani tuxedo—The Look is called a Texas tux.

I remember hearing the great designer Michael Kors say that fashion is only about two things: feeling rich and feeling sexy. It may seem crass to

Dallas by day: A stunning leather minidress, stiletto boots, and lush, wild, big hair.
Dallas by night: Shimmering, svelte, fabulous jewelry—and that hair.

admit, but think about it and tell me that he's wrong. You can't, because he's right—and I think his remark holds true in every small town as well as big city. The Dallas woman especially understands this concept—and dresses beautifully to feel both sexy and rich. And she shops everywhere in her great city.

The new-guard Dallas woman shops in Highland Park Village, where everyone who is anyone shops. There, she searches for the skinny boot-leg, flare, and hipster trousers to wear by day, and there she looks for some serious fashion to wear at night. Instead of TV's *Dallas* style (those beaded, wide-lapel satin suits), which is passé, says the Dallas hairstylist Johnny Johnson, the new-guard Dallas woman thinks *Melrose Place* (those opulent chiffon column dresses). In fact, notes Johnson, "Dallas is really a paradox consisting of Main Street Republicans who dress conservatively, with a hint of sexy, and Main Street Democrats, who dare to be daring, but tailored daring, for the most part—a neckline down to *there* on a wool, pinstripe man-tailored suit."

Many old-guard Dallas women are shabby chic: Hardly anything is ever thrown out, because, my darling, it's *good.* These women go to Deno's, where the staff repairs anything leather—and also creates the most gorgeous custom leather clothing.

Although Dallas is similar to Washington, D.C., in that both are business cities and so they both experience a frequent influx of new blood, they're as different as day from night. In Dallas signs of affluence are everywhere. "Dallas women definitely do dress rich," says the hair-color stylist Richard Hayler, although "there are many who put a lot in the front window but don't have much in the shop." Still, Dallas is a big dress-up city, no matter how much money you have. It's the kind of place where you're *not* about to throw on a pair of shorts and a T-shirt and wander through a department store.

In Dallas, women don't wear day into night, as they do in Washington. Breakfast clothes are to take a breakfast meeting in, tea gowns to have tea in, cocktail clothes to have a martini in, and ball gowns to dance in. Except for black leather, hardly anyone wears black: Gray is about as black as black gets in Dallas.

Finally, comfort counts, but not as much as in, say, Chicago or Atlanta. As one Dallas matron says, "Looking fashionable is key in my world. I like to see things all hanging together, so often I'll buy the outfit—accessories, coat, and all. It's a bonus if it's comfortable, but, you want me to be frank? I won't sacrifice style for comfort."

TIP 1: You get the best cowboy boots at the Western Warehouse.

TIP 2: Chanel is everywhere.

TIP 3: So is money. Daytime diamond studs dot the landscape, as they do in L.A.—not Hope Diamond size, but small jewels that act as flash bulbs lighting up the Dallas woman's face as she plays tennis, shops, or builds her stock portfolio. Most opt for the real thing.

DALLAS STREET SIGNS

- Chanel, Chanel, Chanel. Also Bottega Veneta.
- Cowboy hats, boots, and fringe—the rodeo rides again.
- Whimsical beading on sweaters.
- Red is the chosen color.
- Orange leather minis, feather coats, and go-go boots can be seen at the same club as Calvin Klein's classic tweed jacket and trousers.

GETTING STARTED

Where to start achieving the Big City Look in fashion? One piece at a time is a good place. The woman with The Look uses confidence and panache to pull her wardrobe together . . . *slowly*—seeking out unique and good fabrics, unusual details, and different cuts in design. She's learned how to coordinate new purchases with the wardrobe that currently lives in her closet. She's going for a beautiful look, but mostly she's aiming to be imaginative and interesting. It's precisely that imagination that places her apart, that gives her her special dash—different from that of other well-dressed women in her city.

Know that this dash in every city and small town in America conveys messages, double entendres, nuances, even little white lies, and surely more than can be expressed in mere words about a person. Here are *some* of the things that the imaginative clothes, accessories, and colors you choose can say:

- I'm a winner.
- I'm not available to everyone . . . so keep your distance.
- I'm an original thinker.
- I'm the boss.
- I'm rich and famous.

•I love to take risks, try new things.

•I've got a sense of humor.

You may not really be rich, famous, funny, the boss, or a risk-taking personality—but you have that *effect* on others. The look of the big city implies a certain open-mindedness, a generosity of spirit and imagination, a way of looking at materials, styles, and colors that's just a bit off the beaten track—mixing velvet and denim, for example, or putting a tunic of fine-beaded, whimsical pandas over seriously tailored linen pants. The edgy contradiction makes the fashion stand out.

The Big City Look isn't always on the edge. Overlapping in every big city is another look—an uncluttered, ageless, comfortable kind of chic, a simplicity that reads grown-up, feminine. The look of femininity is definitely back—and it doesn't clash with power.

For example: Nina Griscom, host of the television show *Dining Around*, fashion arbiter Adrienne Vittadini, and songstress Natalie Cole can each put on a classic pair of khaki chinos, sling a cardigan sweater (tie the arms in front, naturally) over a simple, white cotton T, and there it is—The Look! None of these women has perfect features, yet all, with quintessential American style, give a scrubbed-clean, fresh, strong impression.

There's a new approach to sportswear in almost every region. Sweatshirts, parkas, and other athletic wear pop up in unexpected fabrics like parachute silk or organza, making comfort the height of high style.

Break the Rules

Originality is always the most interesting city style. After years of watching and dressing fabulous women, I think that the ones who do it best are filled with a sense of daring. They can make subtle changes depending on their moods—simple one day, edgy the next. They have put in the time experimenting with eccentric, sometimes even chaotic, choices of fashion, rather than settling for the matching shoes, purse, dress of their mothers—even when their moms' clothes were exquisite designer fashions. They translate their personalities and moods into fashion—even when it means breaking rules.

Oh, they break those rules a lot.

Who says, for example, that leather and lace don't "match"? A few nights ago, I saw a client of mine at a charity function, and all eyes were on her: She'd paired a very slim, short silver-lace skirt with a soft, tailored, black leather jacket (a delicate, silver silk camisole peeked out under the jacket), and perched on her shoulder was a tiny, quivering, shivering multi-jeweled hummingbird. There was something about the gorgeous extravagance of that tiny bird, ready to take off from the mannishly attired shoulder, that pulled together the ultrafemininity of the lace and the masculinity of the leather. If the bird had been bigger or the skirt longer or the leather brightly colored, the effect could not have been The Look that turned heads.

Perhaps, in getting started, the easiest way to describe The Look is to tell you what's not The Look. There are *some* rules—six to be exact—that you mustn't break, even if you're a rule breaker at heart.

Too darling for words. That's not The Look. Two hummingbirds would have been too darling. Bows in the hair are too darling. A fringed copper cowboy jacket and a cowboy hat in Washington, D.C., are definitely too darling (not too darling in Dallas, though). Get the picture?

Too much. One soft leather jacket is swell. A leather jacket, leather skirt, leather belt, leather purse, and leather headband shriek excessive, not stylish. A wonderful handknit cardigan is stunning. A handknit cardigan, a hand-painted T-shirt, handmade beads, and a handwoven purse say home-made—in the negative sense of the word. Stick with *one* one-of-a-kind.

Too schizophrenic. I've said that elegant style can pull eccentric elements together, but going overboard makes you appear a bit loony: That's *not* The Look. Mixing three different ethnic looks or an old-fashioned pin with contemporary earrings is confusing rather than pretty. A sequined shirt, a beaded skirt, ten rings, a shawl that clings, and flowered things worn all together are schizophrenic.

Too boring. A camel-colored skirt, camel sweater, camel headband, camel shoes and purse is infinitely boring and is not The Look. Simple is always chic, but you don't want to blend into the landscape and disappear.

Too coordinated. This can get kind of tricky because you do want some coordination—just not too much. For example, test yourself: Which outfit is not too coordinated?

OUTFIT 1
- Black velvet jeans
- Lime-green form-fitting wool sweater
- Black Harris tweed jacket
- Black leather boots
- Multicolored cut-velvet purse (shades of lime, emerald, black, rose)

or

OUTFIT 2

- Black velvet jeans and jacket
- Black and white striped silk shirt
- Black leather pumps
- Black leather shoulder bag

ANSWER: Outfit 1 has The Look—and you know why. Why? Well, both outfits are coordinated, but the first has a surprise—the lime green, of course. Also, the blacks are juxtaposed against the different cut-velvet textures and colors of the purse. Outfit 1 is co-ordinated *and* original. Outfit 2 is coordinated and a bore.

The second outfit is perfectly pretty, perfectly acceptable, and perfectly coordinated, but it misses The Look. It's *too* coordinated, with matching leathers and matching blacks and no imagination.

Not you. Women with The Look may be daring, but they're not chameleons. They stick to their essential selves in fashion. They've discovered what looks best on them. Although they're certainly creative, and make subtle changes in their appearance according to their moods, they rarely deviate from their true type, just because a trend appears in the marketplace. You'll rarely see ruffles or flounces on Diane Sawyer, even off-camera. Her look is sophisticated, tailored—sensational in its simplicity. This is not to say, for example, that an Atlanta woman whose day look consists of muted pastel cashmere sweaters with matching headbands can't dress up at night in a dreamy Chanel gown. Of course she can, and still be authentic, because the Chanel gown is an evening version of her own *classic* Big City Look. If the Atlantan opted for the see-through fishnet dress at the Atlanta ball—a dress that could be outrageously great on a New Yorker—she'd just look silly and unauthentic.

So make your look *you*—and most of the time, make it appropriate to your geography.

Fe Saracino-Fendi wears her family name proudly. With her Fendi cigarette pants and classic Fendi loafers, she shows eclectic New York style simply by leaving the collar of a simple white shirt open down to there and the sleeves unbuttoned. Talk about breaking the rules.

Presentation: A New Fashionable You

Wherever they live, women who have the Big City Look in fashion are women who have learned to make a powerful, credible *presentation*—whether they're on their way to lunch, to a job interview, or to meet their moms. Presentation counts. In America today there is a rare breed of consultant called an *image maker* whose job is to improve your presentation. Bill Clinton has an image maker and most corporate executives have them. Many women who wish to come across as strong, beautiful, and appropriate hire these consultants for considerable fees. A powerful organization, the Association of Image Consultants International, provides lists of such image makers. Consultants suggest hairstylists, appropriate dress, and general advice on how to put yourself together so you look right for the region in which you live. A consultation with an image maker may include color analysis, a closet makeover, and certainly, advice about the kinds of clothes one needs to move gracefully through life.

What follows is your own image consultation: tips and fashion advice, courtesy of Vincent, designed to help you make wardrobe decisions, no matter where you live in this wide land. In selecting your wardrobe, always keep in mind the specific needs of your particular city. While the simple cut of the finest classics—in other words, good taste—remains the same for every city, colors can be counted on to vary from region to region. This means, for example, choosing white or neutral pastels if you live in Atlanta, Los Angeles, or Dallas instead of the darker colors appropriate to colder climes.

Begin with Your Closet

If your everyday closet—not the occasional closet in which you store off-season and unique items—is confusing with its inconsistencies, organize it. That's the first thing you'll hear from even the most expensive image consultant.

Empty the entire closet onto your bed. If you haven't worn an item in two years, be ruthless—it goes to your favorite thrift shop. Put things back in order. Skirts hang with skirts, blouses with blouses, small items like underwear are placed in drawers or in wire or plastic see-through baskets on shelves. Clothes you wear infrequently, such as formal attire, should be placed toward the back of the closet, or in a separate closet. Organizers within the

Actress Kelly Curtis, sister to Jamie Lee Curtis and daughter of Janet Leigh and Tony Curtis, in a zip-up, buttery leather Moschino dress—perfect for Dallas.

closet are also wonderful and can be installed on walls or backs of doors: Hooks, pegs, and an expanding wooden mug rack all work for belts, scarves, purses with chains. Earring racks—frames with wooden bars and holes and slots—neatly hold earrings and other things as well. Closet organizers are available through most mail order catalogues, and especially from a mail order company called Hold Everything (call 800-421-2264 for a catalogue).

Keep It Classic

Now decide what you need to buy—what you *must have* and what you merely crave. It's the *must-haves* we're interested in here, so make a little organized list of what you need in basics: blouses, sweaters, shirts, slacks, power suits, and coats.

Here's the biggest secret: Classics as the basis for the Big City Look go a long way. The classics are then accentuated with such unusual details as bold jewelry or scarves—sometimes just one funky, outrageous touch.

What's a classic? We might as well get this out of the way right now, since you'll be hearing the word a lot.

A classic is an item of clothing that has been around a long time, and is elegant and timeless. Its lines are clean and simple—no extremes, please.

A classic is not trendy (peasant blouses or pillbox hats) or faddish (poodle skirts, white vinyl boots, Nehru jackets). Grunge, which came and went in five minutes, is definitely not classic. Classic is perennial: Your mother could have worn a classic in 1949 and looked as chic in it then as you do today. Think Chanel suits, a cashmere or a Shetland crew-neck sweater, a little black dress, or a simple white cotton shirt.

A classic is usually neutral in color: black, navy, gray, white, off-white, beige, greige. I can't think of too many chartreuse classics.

A classic is made well from good materials—no ugly seams showing, no awkward gathering at the waist. When it comes to fabrics, "classic" doesn't mean heavy and ancient-looking. Classic fabrics can look high-tech and modern and easy-to-wear. Although classic fabrics are usually made from natural fibers—wools (camel-hair, cashmere, Harris tweed), silks, linens, cottons—today some really good synthetics make the grade of classic (rayon, for example). Synthetics that are *not* classics are 100 percent polyester, acrylic double-knits, or fake suedes.

Businesswoman Rosie Moncrief ready for a ball, Texas style—spectacular red gown, spectacular jewelry, spectacular *presence*. (Photogragh © Ray Payne)

Three classic shirts: Notched collar, man-tailored shawl collar, long-sleeved collarless shell.

A classic makes you **look** *rich—old-money rich.* Forgive the political incorrectness, but it's true. Wearing a classic is an in-group signal that says "You're one of us"—affluent, powerful, and tasteful. A classic is a status symbol. You can probably buy good knock-offs of classics—like a Prada purse or a Chanel scarf—on the street, but if they're truly good copies, so what?

What's classic and right for the region sometimes is distinguished by tradition and tiny distinctions. Take jeans. One New Yorker told me that "geeks wear Lees, greaser freaks wear Wranglers, and the truly chic wear only Levi's." Go figure.

The Essentials

Variations of the following belong in every Big City Look wardrobe.

THE SHIRT

Shirts are true staples of any chic wardrobe. Even a boring pair of pants or a nondescript skirt are acceptable when paired with a great shirt. Consider these shirt styles and have at least one or two in solid white and solid black.

Cotton or silk man-tailored, long-sleeved shirts. With a notched collar, perfect under a suit jacket.

Collarless silk shells. Also fine under a jacket.

Silk or jersey shawl-collared shirts. Go great with pants.

Cotton T-shirts. Short- and long-sleeved, in solid colors and stripes, with V-necks, boat necks, crew necks. The newest dressy T's come in bias-cotton, jersey, even cashmere. The little black cotton T with a pair of perfect black trousers is *the* quintessential American city look on a well-toned, long-limbed body. You can't own too many T's. You can't get away with an inexpensive Fruit of the Loom T-shirt, either, especially if you're over forty. Better T's are made from more substantial fabrics that flatter a postforty body. Spring for the pricier Ralph Lauren, Tse, or Jil Sander T.

Silk, crushed-velvet, lace, or ribbed-cotton camisoles. Once thought of only as lingerie, the camisole has shed its underwear label and become a versatile essential in fabrics for day and night. Spaghetti-strapped camisoles look terrific under the appropriate jacket or blouse.

THE SWEATER: MUST-HAVES

Classic turtlenecks. In heavy and light wools or silks and a medley of colors, they work wonderfully with flannel pants or a simple skirt.

A silk or wool knit cardigan. It has infinite uses, and can be worn as a jacket with a stunning blouse underneath or alone and buttoned up, possibly with a knock-out silver choker.

One dressy sweater. At least one dressy sweater should live in your wardrobe. It's usually the fabric (angora, cashmere, crocheted, silk) more than the actual style that makes it slightly more dressy than your everyday cable-knit wool turtleneck. It could have a cowl, crew (or jewel), high V, or boat neck; it could be a lightweight turtleneck or cardigan; it could be sleeveless or have short sleeves. Silk "skinny" sweaters, fine Merino wools with jewel necklines, silk knits or mock turtlenecks go gorgeously under suits.

THE TROUSERS

A pair of simple fly-front pants. In a light summer-/winter-weight wool or wool gabardine, this is the ultimate, go-anywhere style in every wardrobe. The same trousers in dressier fabrics (satin, crepe, velvet) often go to the office as well as the party. The shape of pants changes almost yearly. In some years, narrow-legged, body-skimming pants topped with

Dressier boat-neck sweater
and turtleneck sweater.

shorter jackets are the height of style. In other years, slouchy, wide-legged shapes with longer jackets are the way to go. Read the fashion magazines to see what's in.

Blue jeans. Choose a simple cut, always minus beads and baubles. Worn with a classic blazer, jeans always seem to epitomize The Look.

TIP: The bottom of all pants legs should break on the shoes. Ankles should never be visible.

The incomparable, the brilliant Isabella Rossellini in a simple shawl-collared shirt and pants.
(Photograph © Patrick Demarchelier)

Classic jackets: the blazer, the "Chanel."

THE JACKET

I believe that the jacket is the most important piece of clothing in your wardrobe. It's bankable style, the fashion item first noticed on that stunning woman passing by. Jackets complement shorts, jeans, pants, skirts, dresses—anything you choose for the bottom. I love a somewhat broader shoulder in a jacket. Lined jackets look richest and hold their shape best. Longer jackets go best with pants, shorter with skirts. Women with big hips look best in long jackets with high closures. Those with narrow waists look best in a jacket with a one-button closure. And women with large bosoms look best in unstructured jackets with no lapels.

TIP 1: Look closely—does your outfit cut you in equal halves? If so, fix it. It's wrong. Long jackets should be paired with straight pants or skirts, and

short, cropped jackets should be paired with flared or wide-legged pants—
or even straight, long dresses.

TIP 2: It's not engraved in stone anywhere that you have to wear something
under the jacket, but bare skin looks best with a sleek-lines suit.

In your closet should hang at least one or two of these options:

The clean-lined, notch-collared blazer.

A Chanel-type jacket—pockets and all. The typical Chanel-type
jacket was always worn as part of a suit, but it's a great look paired with
velvet or silk pants and chunky-heeled shoes.

A long jacket. Collarless, with a round or V neck.

A long cardigan. Functions well as a jacket.

THE SUIT

A suit is nothing more than a jacket and skirt that match, but the suit has
its own niche, especially for the working woman. It has always made great
sense to wear a strong suit to the office, because suits mean business.
Today's suits, with their exquisite tailoring and fine fabrics, are, however,
quite different from those your mom wore to her office. The best suits today
have looser, longer jackets and retain a feeling of femininity despite having
broader shoulders. No longer little uniforms, suits can easily take a woman
from office to evening by means of a simple quick change of shirts and
shoes as darkness falls. Sometimes the quick change involves wearing no
shirt at all and just relying on a little cleavage for high style.

THE SKIRT

Although the "prison-matron" skirt length, ending well below the knee,
periodically becomes a buzzword for big city style, shorter skirts always
eventually save the day. Why? Skirts should be built for speed. Most women
with The Look don't have time for the mincing, tiny steps that slim *long*
skirts require. Don't even choose a full, awkwardly long skirt, which seems
matronly, or a too-full short skirt, which looks childish. Here are some classics: buy one or more to blend with the shirt colors you've chosen.

The A-line skirt. This style moves best; it's a slim fit and works fine
with a tucked-in shirt.

The narrow, slim-line skirt. It is stunning and built for speed,
because today's version—and that may include a longer skirt—has pleats or
slits for striding ease.

The short or long pleated skirt. Pleated styles work well with a long
or short jacket.

Three dress styles: the wrap, the shirt dress, the long chemise.

The miniskirt. The mini deserves a special word. It's so versatile. For example, there are three hundred ways to wear a black mini: Try it with an oversize turtleneck and knee-high riding boots or a fitted dressy turtleneck with higher heels; try it under a long camel-hair coat or under a short, jewel-color leather jacket; try it with a simple T-shirt and high-tech sneakers or with a black stretch gabardine top and knee-high boots. If you are over forty, be reasonable: Don't go too short. If you are under forty, go short.

Finally, the evening skirt. Evening skirts are great night-time mix-

Actress/director Joanna Kerns in a tailored white tuxedo with her daughter Ashley Kerns in power black-and-white Calvin Klein pinstripes. Classics rule.

and-matchers; the color, fabric, and length determine just how formal your look will be. A long velvet or satin skirt with a high slit is always sensual. Paired with a stunning silk or satin blouse, or a formal jacket—perhaps with rhinestone or bead buttons—or a slinky halter top, or even an evening sweater, the effect is pure dynamite and can go anywhere, from the theater or opera to a wedding.

A rich, midcalf wool or tweed skirt paired with a classic wool blazer is less dressy but perfect for dinner or the theater. A short tulip-hem skirt paired with a bare, strippy-strap silky top is delicious for a tryst.

THE DRESS

The classic coatdress. A daytime wardrobe staple in a tailored-looking fabric—perhaps solid or pinstripe wool for winter, striped cotton for summer—goes everywhere alone or under a jacket, dressed up or down with appropriate jewelry.

The chemise. A straight-up-and-down look, sometimes curving in slightly at the waist, in a solid-color wool or crepe that can be dressed up or down with accessories. Because it's so simple, it must be very well made.

The knit. Their texture ranging from cashmere and felt wool jersey to soft and silky mohair, knit dresses and suits are *always* appropriate in daylight and even moonlight hours.

TIP 1: Dress fabrics that are especially wonderful for the Big City Look on cool days: soft camel-hair, cashmere, suede, and tweed.
TIP 2: I like *some* structure in dresses. Unless you're nineteen years old, a dress shouldn't cling to every part of your body or just hang there, shapelessly.

The evening dress. A marvelously simple slip or wrap dress (long or short) in silk or silk jersey is always pretty and appropriate. Naturally, an evening jacket can be added. I believe that simplicity in evening dresses is the way to go. Anything too elaborate takes away from the essential you—the dress wears you instead of you wearing the dress. If you have the need for it, one perfectly lovely evening gown is a divine addition to an evening wardrobe—perhaps a pencil-thin pleated column punctuated with a thigh-high slit for the adventurous; perhaps a Chinese mandarin–style brocade shift, long or short; perhaps a distinguished designer gown. Buy a classic, buy it carefully. It will last for years. If you can't afford an exquisite gown,

I can't resist grabbing Liz Smith for a quick dance. All Texans—even power-suited ones, even transplanted ones—like to party.

pump

stacked heel oxford

high-heel sandal

backless pump

espadrille

pantsuit boot

hiking boot

try haunting the fabric shops for seconds or remnants of a magnificent fabric. A local dressmaker can whip up a copy of a designer gown you love for a fraction of the cost. Provide a photo to make your wishes clear.

A rule of thumb for interesting evening wear is: *Keep it uncomplicated, keep it comfortable, mix it up.* For instance, wear a contemporary necklace with a vintage gown).

THE UNDERWEAR

Comfort reigns. Buy beautiful bras—but not if they cut into your shoulders or midriff, thereby installing a permanent grimace on your face. Sport bras are marvelous for everyday wear as well as for sports activities.

Use street smarts when choosing underwear. Panty lines under slacks, for example, are très gauche.

Here's the prime point: Even if no one sees your underwear, *you* know what you have on in those wonderfully secret places. Delicately lacy, beautifully patterned, comfortable underwear gives you a longer, more confident, big city stride. Believe it! And certainly, pull out all the stops in the evening—even if you're the only one to know you have on a hundred-dollar lace push-up bra. You *should* feel glamorous when the moon is out. Go for it.

THE LEGWEAR

The fashion designer Donna Karan says that great legwear is as important as any other fashion item. "Clothes can be sexy, but if a woman doesn't feel sexy underneath, what's the use? With matte jerseys, skinny knits, and layered sheers, with hemlines as variable as they are, no one can deny how important a pair of hose is."

I agree. Try pantyhose in classic invisible sheers and the palest of beiges for light outfits and the sheerest darker shades for dark suits and dresses. Never wear black stockings with a white dress and white shoes—or vice versa. Bare feet or sandaltoed hose must always be worn with sandals. Choose either delicately textured or heavier ribbed pantyhose under short wool skirts and pantsocks in every color to blend with your trousers.

THE SHOES

This is the most important advice about shoes you'll ever hear: They can't be cheap. Bad-quality shoes are a sure sign to everyone that you don't understand The Look.

Low versus high heels? I have to repeat what one Washington woman told me. "The first thing anyone who loves high heels has to admit," she

Fe Saracino-Fendi in a classic sleeveless evening shift made memorable by the fabric— hand-beaded, 18-karat-gold- thread embroidered silk. Very *Gilda*/Rita Hayworth.

said, "is the sense of power you get when you feel taller." It's true and the woman with The Look in every American region likes the feeling of being strong. Perhaps there are women who harbor a genuine affection for the *feel* of pointy toes and spindly heels—but they're rare, and most orthopedists tell us that really high heels are murder on the back. Still, it's The Look many women *and* men love, and even those who find high heels uncomfortable tend to grin and bear them for the sake of style on special occasions (often compromising by opting for a larger size to ease their toes).

The term "high heels" may include spikes or chunky or tapered heels, depending on the fashion trend of the year. Higher heels do seem to add clout to dressing up—not to mention the wonderfully flattering things they do for legs. In the end, Manolo Blahnik's open-sided pump with a three-inch heel and an ankle strap is either heaven or hell—depending on who's walking in it.

For day wear, low heels and fine leather flats certainly are also stylish, especially with dressy trousers. If you don't have a pair of classic pumps in good black, brown, or sandy leather or suede, you're in trouble. A stunning pair of luggage-colored, stacked-heel oxfords or Joan and David's lace-up buttery leather boots for really sporty occasions are very useful. When you're ready to play, dig into the closet for J. P. Tod's leather loafers with the rubber heels, the Nike Air Zoom cross-trainers, the Timberland hiking boots. In spring and summer, the sling-backs, black and white spectators (the Chanel sling-back version of the spectator is the classic), espadrilles, and sandals are always seen in the big city.

For the evening, if you do love the look of higher heels, you should own a pair black or chocolate silk, faille, velvet, or satin pumps or sling-backs to go with a myriad of dressy outfits. Those whose comfort zone absolutely depends on flat or low heels somehow manage to find stunning ones that perfectly complement the evening wear they've chosen. If you have doubts, ask a personal shopper or a salesperson to suggest the perfect shoe for the outfit.

For dressing-up, it must be said that absolutely nothing is more beautiful than those Manolo Blahnik's spikes. But not everyone can manage the height—not to mention the price!—of the prettiest spikes. In general, the simpler the shoe and the better the shoe material, the better the look. A graceful, medium-high black satin pump or sandal is always wonderful. Another look that is wonderful for evening wear is high-heel sling-backs,

One simple, classic, exquisite gown by Versace is all anyone needs. Of course, it helps to look like the model Silke.

Television star Nina Griscom is outstandingly Big City in her elegant Donna Karan gown and her strappy evening sandals by Yves St. Laurent. Check out the fine hosiery by Fogal, crucially important in a dress with a slit like this one! Her honey-blond hair (with chunky platinum streaks) is gathered high in a large, simple clip.

dusted with beads and baubles, à la Isaac Mizrahi or Gucci. Strippy evening sandals, available in steel-color, gold, bronze, or clear, also surprisingly come in handy and are so much lovelier than the old-fashioned dyed-to-match-the-gown pumps, which are really not considered stylish anymore—not anywhere.

TIP 1: Always try to tone (not match) shoes to your clothes, purse, and/or belt.

TIP 2: The fancier the shoe (bows, beads, sparkles), the more your eye is drawn to the leg. Overly decorated shoes tend visually to shorten leg length.

TIP 3: If you don't have enough money for a great pair of everyday shoes *and* great boots, always go for the boots. Enough cannot be said for boots. They're more visible, they don't go out of style as quickly as shoes, and they last longer. In many regions, including the warmer ones, many women with The Look wear boots all year round. They lend verve to pants and both short and long skirts. Mannish shoes are a version of boots.

THE PURSE

Here's the thing about purses: As with shoes, you can never wear cheap ones and look stylish. A cheap purse stands out like a sore thumb. Good handbags are made of the best, most supple materials, with linings that match the color of the purse. The stitches, even in the strap, should be uniform and close to invisible. The bag should open and close fluidly. Any metallic touches on the bag or strap should have a fine, burnished hue and not look brassy, flashy, gaudy, or cheap.

Purses fall victim to the year's latest trends, but a few classics always remain in style. These classics are often reproduced inexpensively but so well that the deception is almost impossible to detect. Some oft-copied classics are the quilted, tasseled, gold-chained, over-the-shoulder Chanel purse, Louis Vuitton's tote bags, and the Hermès "Kelly" (after Grace Kelly) Bag with handles. The classics—or very good imitations of the classics—always lend The Look. Your purse doesn't have to match your shoes as long as they're in the same tone.

Some points:

Your handbag should be constructed of the best leather, suede, or fabric you can afford. The most practical leather often has a subtle pattern that hides wear and tear. Even when it comes to summer straw purses, there are the cheaply made ones and then there are the wonderful, tightly

She's stunning and feminine in her Ungaro pink plaid jacket—but don't mess with New York State's Westchester County District Attorney Jeanine Pirro. You'll lose. The Big City Look goes hand in hand with power. The functional, fabulous Hermès purse is part of the look. Shoes by Prada.

woven versions. Always spend a few more dollars and get the better bag. It shows.

Before you purchase a handbag, think proportion. Your sporty, everyday purse should be beautiful *and* functional—big and with enough compartments to allow quick retrieval of the items you need but not so huge as to throw your look off balance or so tiny as to look silly. A too-long purse can also throw your proportions off.

Instead of an ungainly, enormous purse, carry an additional tote or workbag for lugging work back and forth to the office. Here to stay, and taking the place of the tote, are stunning leather or fabric backpacks. Dooney & Bourke and Coach put out splendid leather models that are chic, utilitarian, easy on the back—and also readily available in big city street knock-offs, I might add. Most recently—another example of street smarts going high fashion—we now have messenger chic. The messsenger bag has been co-opted by designers like Armani, Kate Spade, and Gucci in trendy leather and nylon.

- When it comes to bags, probably all you need in life is:
  —a good everyday leather shoulder bag like the Coach bag, which goes with everything, winter and summer.
  —a stunning heavy-gauge nylon or cotton tote or a knapsack, Prada or Gucci style.
  —a smaller evening purse that works with every outfit, in a colorless metallic bronze or silver gray, depending on the tone of your evening shoes. You might also consider the classic flat envelope bag in black or brown satin or silk, which blends well with many outfits.
- This is how experts say a purse should be worn:
  —If it has a very long strap, wear it over one shoulder, then sling it across your body so it rests on your hipbone.
  —If it has a medium-long strap, wear it close to but not across your body.
  — A clutch purse should be held at its center. Incidentally, the multicolor, convertible clutch with a removable shoulder strap is marvelously adaptable. Wear it to the office with the strap. Remove the strap for evening.
  —A handle bag should be held by the handle, not with the handle slung over the forearm, Queen Elizabeth style.
- A few words about briefcases:
  —The Big City Look translates into authority with a stunning

leather briefcase, but remember that cases no longer *have* to be leather to be smart.

—Fabric totes from catalogue kings like L. L. Bean are also terrific, lightweight, and fine for holding unwieldy hair dryers, makeup kits, and reams of manuscript paper—as well as a courtroom brief.

—If you're going to have The Look, swing that briefcase with authority—with *attitude*—as you stride down Michigan Avenue, Madison Avenue, Pennsylvania Avenue, or your own avenue in your own big city.

THE COAT

Coats have come into their own. They're no longer just functional items but are prime building blocks of any fashionable wardrobe. An everyday coat should be of stellar design: A camel-hair chesterfield, a double-breasted wool melton, or a belted gabardine trench coat are classic choices.

Most free-spirited women pay little attention to trends in coat hemlines and have several coats in many lengths to suit their own moods and wardrobes. Ankle-length coats are striking and lend dash to pants and minimal minis. Pea-coat length, knee-length, and thigh-high coats are perfect for short skirts.

My all-time favorite? A roomy, slightly-longer-than-midcalf coat that comes in many styles, including a bathrobe, wrap, or cape-coat. It looks equally wonderful over pants or long *and* short skirts.

In colder climates like Chicago, New York, and Washington, short coats and pea jackets are key players for chic, casual overwear. Long, slim-lined, ungimmicky single- or double-breasted coats lend The Look everywhere. In warmer climes—Atlanta, Dallas, Los Angeles—denim or polished cotton for daylight and silk for evening are great coat choices. In even warmer climes, oversize scarves and shawls *are* coats. And don't forget capes: The most exciting-looking woman I ever saw was wrapped in a black velvet cape.

Every city woman has a city slicker in her wardrobe. Chic women wear raincoats even when it's not raining—*especially* when it's not raining. From the classic yellow "fisherman" slicker to the traditional buttoned Burberry, raincoats go everywhere from the office to the theater.

It's also helpful to have a stunning, goes-anywhere, more formal wrap stowed in your closet. Many women spend copious amounts of time

California socialite Denise Hale in a majestic, cardinal-red, roomy coat.

choosing just the right evening outfits but totally forget the dressier cover-up, and they end up staring hopelessly at the navy-blue pea coat two minutes before departure time. That wonderful black velvet cape, a boa wrap or jacket, a fringed silk shawl, a simple satin evening coat are fine wrap possibilities.

Vincent's Three Wardrobe Must-Haves
THE UBIQUITOUS LITTLE BLACK DRESS

I don't even have to ask. But if I did ask about the most favorite fashion of all, many of my clients would swear by a simple black sheath, or a variation of it: the universally delicious little black dress. Coco Chanel invented it in 1926 for women who want to look simple, sexy, and powerful, and ever since then there has been a little black dress in their closets. I guarantee it: The woman with the Big City Look owns one. In her book devoted entirely to the little black dress, Amy Holman Edelman concludes, "The garment is shorthand for chic; it's a loaded fashion symbol."

Designers at all price levels always try to tempt women to abandon the little black dress, with little success: The little black dress with its slimming elegance and unmatchable practicality will always be immensely popular with the chicest urban dwellers. Women love the little black dress because it makes them look svelte, because it makes them feel self-assured without looking as if they tried too hard, because it lends an air of mystery, confidence, and, yes, sex. The little black dress may stay little—but today it comes in infinite varieties. During the day, look for a simple little black wool A-line on the most beautiful woman moving assuredly around Washington's Dupont Circle, up New York's Fifth Avenue, and down Chicago's Michigan Avenue. In the evening, look for a little black beaded slip-dress on a Dallas stunner, a long-sleeved cocktail version on an Atlanta beauty, and Diane von Furstenberg's slinky black velvet wrap on an L.A. starlet. You choose. It's a must-have.

SOMETHING IN LEATHER

"Do I feel sexy in this? Do I feel rich in this?" are the unspoken questions almost every woman asks herself—politically correct or not. Well, having something in really good leather in your wardrobe is about feeling both sexy and rich. If it's of the finest quality, luxurious, butter-soft, leather is won-

Texas-born Phyllis George, former Miss America, former first lady of Kentucky, and present New York entrepreneur, in a come-hither little black dress—relieved by a slice of a slash below the neck. Fashion by Erreuno.

New York on the edge: Kelly
Curtis in an excellent
Moschino black leather skirt,
black leather boots, and
black silk camisole. Wow.

derful. If it strays even a millimeter from the finest quality, forget leather—it will scream tacky. How can you tell "butter-soft"? Go to the best department store in your region, find the designer leathers, and touch them. They should be soft and supple. Then go to an "everything for twenty dollars" store. Touch the leather skirt or vest hanging on the rack. You'll see.

Good leather is available today in slim sheath dresses, whole suits, short skirts, and pants in jewel colors (red, yellow, green, pewter) as well as blacks and browns. And nothing makes us feel so totally cool as a racy leather jacket— remember Marlon Brando in *The Wild One*? Fine leather has impact.

ONE "ALWAYS-WORKS" OUTFIT

It's essential to have in your wardrobe one outfit in which you always feel comfortable, one outfit to grab when you don't have time to think "Oh God, what can I wear?" For many women, the "always-works" outfit consists of a pair of perfect black slacks in velvet, satin, or silk, paired with *anything*—a cashmere cardigan, a cable-knit turtleneck, an outrageously colored organza blouse, a sharply tailored, expensive white shirt. In warmer climes, white or sherbet-colored pants substitute for the black version.

It always works.

HOW TO SHOP IN A DEPARTMENT STORE

I'm a lucky man. Here, at the apex of what has been an extraordinary career, I'm grateful to be affiliated with a legendary department store. I have a client who told me that when she was a teenager in Menasha, Wisconsin, her dream was to visit New York—not to see the Empire State Building or the Statue of Liberty, but to walk through the doors of Saks Fifth Avenue. Who could blame her? The store is a *destination*—a mecca for shoppers who seek not only the traditional classics but the most contempo-

Something in leather: butter-soft, licorice leather from head to toe—there's a look.

rary, advanced fashion. It's a *hip* place to be—both in spirit and merchandise, and children of all ages have as much fun here as they do at the circus. There's a sense of adventure in this place.

Which brings me to the next section of this book. Across the country, in or near most big cities, are many, fine department stores. You can keep your tiny, exclusive, overpriced, limited boutiques—give me a great department store to fill the needs of a busy person who cares about looking city-chic.

But there's an art and a craft to shopping at Saks—and at other large department stores—an inside track that the savvy know how to run. Those who can cleverly tackle a big city department store inevitably end up with the best Big City Look for the best value.

A client comes into my salon in Saks Fifth Avenue and gets the short haircut of her dreams. It's not enough, she tells me, now she feels she has nothing to wear. She's a terribly insecure shopper and really needs some help putting together the fashion appropriate for the new hairstyle. Her biggest shopping problems come because most department stores are so daunting in their bigness. How do you know where to go for what? How do you navigate an endless maze of linked boutiques?

Do I really love this client? If I do, I may tell her to meet me early in the morning before the store officially opens for a lesson in zipping through a huge department store with Zen-like focus. Together we'll find her look.

I can't do the same with every reader of this book, but what follows are some of the things I'd teach you if I could personally walk you through the store.

Make a Little List

First, draw up a little list of priorities. Do you need a shirt for the navy suit, an evening wrap, a black sweater for work? Now that your hair is short, would a turtleneck sweater look better than the boat necks you've always worn? Keep the priorities list short. You're just learning.

Now, with list in hand, the first thing to do is . . .

Play "Just Looking, Thank You"

Before professional shoppers make even one suggestion to their clients, they cruise the territory to know what's available. They want to have an idea of the offerings in most of the major departments in a store. In the back of their minds they've registered the interesting blazers on three and the marvelous rain slicker on five, and they don't even want to think about the bizarre outfits in department "X" on the second floor. They have a general merchandise map in their heads telling them what's what, and where.

So cruise the store in order to have your own merchandise map in your head. Ride the escalators to get a visual picture of the lay of the land. Get a printed store directory and make notes on it: "The great shoes in my price range were on three. The angora sweater was over there on five."

Leave Your Credit Card at Home

Remember, you're not to buy one thing—yet. You're *just looking*. Along with the store directory, it's helpful to carry a small notebook to jot down interesting things that catch your eye. Some tips:

- Wear comfortable shoes but bring a pair of heels. If you eventually plan to wear heels with any garment, you'll need them for trying on to get an accurate effect.
- Forget your ingrained shopping hangups—it's too expensive, too brightly colored, too short—because you're not spending money at this point—you're *just looking*. You're here to experiment, open your eyes to new possibilities, and you're definitely going to try on things you've never tried before.
- Cruise the department store on a day when your hair looks terrific and the clothes you're wearing give you confidence. *Just looking* on a bad-hair day defeats every purpose.
- Familiarize yourself with the store's *best* merchandise. Even if you've never before shopped in a more expensive couture department, go there now. Don't be intimidated by cool-acting salespeople. They're hired to help you.

Think of Your Role Model

In the chapter on hair, I explained how helpful it is to choose a role model whose hairstyle you admire. When shopping, do the same thing. Think of a woman who has great fashion style. Then put yourself in her shoes for an hour. You're not going to really copy her—just educate yourself to possibilities you never before considered.

Would Barbara choose this stunning yellow suit? Would she consider that unusual textured brocade vest to go with it? Could you conceive of her blending the yellow of the suit with a leopard-print blouse—even if, to you, it seems like a loony combination? If the answer is yes to any of the ideas you come up with, *consider* the outfit for yourself.

If you can really visualize Barbara in the suit, but the bright yellow color, while great on her, makes you look like a hepatitis victim, look for the same suit in a different color. After a while, as you think about choosing fashions with a specific, chic woman in mind, you'll begin to see yourself as the chic woman. You'll begin to be more selective, disregarding what's right for her but wrong for you. Eventually, you'll develop a personal style that's uniquely you—with a little help from Barbara—or the unique Julia Ormond, if she's your chosen role model.

Observe the Rich

Money doesn't buy taste or big city style, but often the very rich buy the services of professionals who do have taste and style. So sit down in the restaurant of a wonderful department store, order a salad, and check out the wealthy ladies who lunch. You're doing research. See how monied people express fashion elegance.

Ask yourself, "Would that embroidered sweater be smashing on me, or is it a tad tacky—no matter how expensive it probably was?" Or you might think, "I'm going to look for a blazer—and pair it with slacks just like those on that stunning brunette."

It takes time and observation to develop an eye for style. Play the looking game for a day or so. Amble through every interesting department—just as though you were visiting a museum. At home, in the evenings, read the best fashion magazines to get an idea of high style. Perhaps high style is not *your* style, but be able to recognize the trends in department stores when you spot them.

Make Friends with the Men's Department

Don't limit yourself to women's wear.

There's a sea change in fashion, a new symbiosis between men's and women's wear that looks as if it will last because it makes *sense.* Many top designers, like Jil Sander, Giorgio Armani, Helmut Lang, and Ralph Lauren, design clothes for men and women with hardly any discernible differences except cut. In their designs, men and women share the same narrow pants (with the woman perhaps using a man's tie to *belt* her pants), the flat-front trousers, the shorter, closer-to-the-body, narrower-in-the-shoulder jackets. Of course, savvy women add their unique touches—a great scarf, fabulous earrings, *something*—to mark the difference in gender. Today, the world of fashion is definitely not split in half between men and women, and

Julia Ormond, the picture of relaxed elegance. (Photograph © Sante D'Orazio)

both sexes take advantage of the overlaps when shopping.

I don't know the reason for it, but often, great sweaters, shirts, belts, socks—you name it—are less costly in the men's department, and that holds true for other items, too. If comfort dressing figures high on your list, an item in a small men's size may fit you even more wonderfully than the medium you usually take in the women's department. If you like something, try it on. In this age of androgynous dressing, give yourself another whole set of department-store shopping tools by including—rather than exclud-ing—men's and even children's departments for some items. Browse at least—what have you got to lose?

Department Store Catalogues Point the Way

There's a reason why a certain combination of separates or an interesting piece of ethnic jewelry makes its way onto the cover of a department-store catalogue: The buyers for the store thought it was great. So browse in the store catalogues for good ideas. If you can afford the exact item you covet, terrific. If not, you can often duplicate fashion ideas by buying similar but less expensive items in a less costly department. You'd love that simple, stunning blazer you see on page 3 of the catalogue but its couture price makes you dizzy? Take the catalogue to a floor that's not couture and ask a salesperson, who knows her merchandise, "Do you have something similar to this?" You'll be amazed at your discoveries.

Take It with You

Clients tell me that as they shop for an outfit, they feel uncomfortable taking an item from one department to match it to something on another floor. That's a big mistake. It's almost always policy in a good department store to allow items to travel from floor to floor. Ask a salesperson first, of course. If the answer is yes, don't hesitate to take the perfect plum scarf on the third floor up to the dress with touches of perfect plum on the sixth floor to make sure the combination works. Also, what looks like soft, perfect plum in the store may turn out to be garish purple when you get it home and match it to the dress in your closet. It's only fair and proper to return what you don't want to its proper home—but I didn't have to tell you that.

Cross over the Bridge

Don't for a minute think that great-looking women always pay top dollar for their clothes. They don't. Designer fashions are swell but often prohibitively expensive. So street smarts tell you to think "bridge" as you shop in the department stores. It's a word coined by retailers to describe style priced to bridge the gap between couture and affordable designer fashion. Today almost every designer has a bridge line that stresses comfort and fit along with the same design sensibility as higher-priced couture. For example, these designer bridge lines—Anne Klein II (Anne Klein), DKNY (Donna Karan), Emanuel (Ungaro), Isaac (Isaac Mizrahi), CK (Calvin Klein), Ralph

All those famous designer names—do they belong to real people? Most of the time. Here's Adrienne Vittadini with her husband, GiGi, on the terrace of their New York apartment. Note the shades—always important for the look. Also check out the gorgeous cable-knit sweater—her own design, naturally.

Comfort rules: The look is often athletic and comfortable in big cities. Here's actress Wendy Waring in shades, Nikes, and Ralph Lauren sports togs doing her city jog and stretch.

(Ralph Lauren), and Kors (Michael Kors)—are all less expensive than the designers' traditional lines, but they still incorporate much of the fine tailoring, fabrics, and style of the higher-priced versions.

Get Your Own Personal Shopper

By the way, personal shoppers for your own use are available in most department stores, certainly here in Saks Fifth Avenue—gratis! Some women prefer to go it alone, but if you think you need professional advice, think about contacting the store's personal shopper department; call the store's information services. I certainly wouldn't advise using a personal shopper every time you need a pair of shoes, but if you're changing your look or are making a big splurge, professional advice is really nice. Asking a personal shopper for advice is different from asking a salesperson. Personal shoppers usually don't make commissions on the items they sell.

Never feel you have to buy anything just because a salesperson or personal shopper has spent time with you. Unless you love it, don't buy it.

Once you've cruised the store for one or two days, it's time to gather up your charge card or your checkbook and set out to shop, my friend.

Put Blinders On

Today, you're psyched for business.

Number one on your list is a costly black cashmere sweater. But you can't afford it. Your mission? Find a less costly look-alike. Look in every sweater-carrying department. Don't be sidetracked by shoes, don't be stopped by lingerie—pass 'em by. Let your blinders blind you to everything but sweaters. See the skirts? No skirts! *Go for sweaters.* A black sweater. Only.

You can't find the *exact* style of that smashing black cashmere? This black wool sweater over here has the same length you admired, the same neckline—and those great shoulders the other sweater didn't even have. Would it work over your evening skirt? Yes? Try it. Buy it.

Enlist the Salesperson's Support

A client of mine once coveted an Armani tuxedo suit that she couldn't afford. She tried it on—it fit perfectly. She asked the salesperson if she could possibly be called when the Armani went on sale. Yes, it was possible. She got the prize at half the price.

A few words on salespeople. They really can make your life easier if you can get them to think of your needs as their needs. Sometimes it's as simple as talking to them gently and warmly—believe it or not, few shoppers do. A grin, a "Good morning," even a warm touch encourages a salesperson to give you directions regarding size, where to find merchandise, and the characteristics of the clothes you're interested in. But be careful. The savvy shopper doesn't depend on the salesperson's opinion of how terrific she looks in the clothes. Even if the salesperson means well, face it—her deepest interest is in pushing a sale to get a commission. Rely on your own judgment or take a trusted friend along for an unbiased opinion.

Shop the Sales

Department stores run great, legitimate sales. If your money is tight, ask for the store's sales schedule. Also, after the sale, and as the season wears down, clothes will be reduced even further. You'll do far better obtaining style, quality, and great prices at a department-store sale than you would at a discount store. Sometimes I see the most *gorgeous* bargains during sales. This week I noticed an exquisite two-hundred-dollar silk blouse in Saks marked down to *fifty* dollars! Beat that.

Many department stores also have "outlet centers," places where their own marvelous merchandise is always available at a fraction of the cost. Ask and Ye Shall Find.

Some stores offer sneak previews of sales. If you're on a mailing list, you'll be advised of these. Try to window-shop the night before a sale starts and observe the salespeople putting out the sale items on the racks. The next morning, to get first choice, run, don't walk, to the sale item you *must* have.

If a great sales item doesn't fit, alter it. Most stores have alterations services. Don't bring home the gorgeous bargain designer dress with the waistline that would cover China. Even if getting the alteration costs more—and ask to see how much more it would cost to alter that waist—it's no bargain if it doesn't fit.

Be a Preferred Customer

You can be a member of an exclusive group of shoppers who receive red-carpet treatment at your favorite department store. Many stores, including Saks, Dayton's, Hudson's, Marshall Field's, K Mart, and JC Penney, offer preferred-customer clubs, but few people are even aware of them. The clubs have different requirements and offer all kinds of perks, which may include gift certificates, free local delivery, cash rebates, previews of sales events, and more. At Saks Fifth Avenue the club is called SaksFirst, and all you have to do to receive the perks is charge two thousand dollars' worth of merchandise annually or pay a fifty-dollar fee.

Free Advice

People whose business is beauty are usually good at fashion. If you have a favorite hair or makeup stylist in the department store, it's not a bad idea to bring your clothes choices to that person when he or she has a free moment and ask an opinion—as do many of my clients in Saks. In fact, I'd be offended if a client needed help and didn't ask. Use the department store and all of its services as your resource.

STREET SMARTS

The Comfort Zone

In defining elegance, one must never forget comfort and quality. Let's look first at comfort.

Most great-looking women with The Look instinctively believe there is a mind-body connection. According to a recent Roper Poll, 94 percent of all American women are convinced that physical comfort and mental well-being are closely connected—and that both figure strongly in looking terrific.

They're right. You can't develop that chic city look unless you feel jaunty and comfortable. You rarely see a chic woman bopping along in the city with a pinched face. How can you look dreamy if you hurt—and we're not talking only about spike heels.

We're also talking body language. When you move, your clothing moves as well—and sends out messages ("I'm uncomfortable and clumsy"—or "I'm at ease and secure"). The best fashion allows your body to speak with comfort and confidence. Always think of how your body will move when you choose your clothes. For example:

- If the pockets of a jacket are too high, you can't stand at ease with one or both hands dipped into the pockets.
- If a skirt or pants lining is cheap and cut tightly, you'll bend funny, and just forget about how you'll look getting out of a low chair!
- If a sleeve is too short or too tight, you'll look ungainly when you have to reach for something or bend down to retrieve a dropped lipstick.
- If your belt is too tight or too high, it restricts movement. If it's placed too low on your body, your hip movements will have to compensate—and will look ungainly. Practice moving in front of the mirror—*after* you put on your belt.

Comfortable big city style doesn't only mean sweatpants and jogging shoes. The most stunning clothes are also designed in materials that help you move easily through all parts of your life: jersey, cotton, and cotton duck in the summertime; featherweight swingy wools, gabardine, and corduroys in the fall; knits and heavier wools in the winter. "I think of it this way," says one Chicago jewelry designer. "I put on a new outfit, and if I can't drive, bend, walk, and turn at least one guy's head in the length of a city block, I don't wear it again."

Don't be a fashion victim, please! If it cuts, binds, tickles, chafes, rubs, or squeezes, it's not street smart to wear it and it won't even look good.

COMFORT TIPS

- High-style layering can be grossly uncomfortable for some. A shirt-sleeve stuck under a lined jacket sleeve caught under a shawl can drive you nuts. Layer with caution.
- Check out the way clothes are made. Bulky linings that impede movement? Pass them by. An underwire bra that digs deep? Pass it by.
- Binding armholes and slim-shaped jackets can make life miserable. Include fashion designed from the new stretch fibers like Lycra and Supplex. They accommodate the body.
- The shoes are *perfect*—except they kill you? I think you should just say no—although you might make exceptions for special evenings if they're not *ridiculously* uncomfortable and you won't be wearing them for too long. You *could* try one of those liquid-filled comfort shoe liners put out by Dr. Scholl.
- Your shoulder bag holds everything, but the strap gives you a back-ache? Look for a bag with a shorter, wider strap, or a backpack with shoulder padding.
- Your pantyhose binds at the waist? Many brands now offer wider waistbands that don't pinch or curl.

The Quality Quotient

Once comfort is assured in fashion, street-smart women focus in on quality, and it is said that here, *God is in the details*. It's those details that make an outfit stylishly chic or ordinary. Here are some details worthy of attention:

Buttons. Good buttons and well-made buttonholes make a suit in okay, inexpensive fabric look like a suit in fine, costly fabric. *Great* buttons make the suit look like couture. Look for clean, thread-free buttonholes that fit the buttons well. If you love a particular jacket but think it has ordinary buttons, change them. In most big cities, vintage or one-of-a-kind button stores are listed in the Yellow Pages under "Buttons." Good buttons are expensive but are worth every penny.

Coat-pocket placement. The lower the pocket, the more elegant the coat. Bet on it.

Armhole size. Armholes cut too high or too skimpily mark a jacket or dress as cheap.

Lining. Nothing marks an inferior garment as quickly as a poorly made or frayed lining. A quality lining feels luxurious, not thin and papery. In quality coats, the coat hem is caught to the lining hem. If the lining hangs completely free, the coat construction is probably not terrific.

Thread. If a coat or dress is hemmed with clear plastic thread, beware. This stitching pulls out quickly and is a clue that the manufacturer probably took shortcuts elsewhere.

Drape. Drape is the way a garment falls on your body—and that should be graceful and flowing, not stiff. Take silk, for example: Just because a label says the garment is 100 percent silk doesn't mean the fabric is excellent. You can tell by the drape whether silk is of good quality. Good silk flows almost like liquid over the body. Every fabric should have supple drape.

Seams. When buying clothes with plaids, stripes, or large patterns, make sure the pattern is well matched at the seams.

Zipper. A properly set zipper should lie flat and even. If it puckers or curls, it's a clue that the whole garment has been hastily put together.

What's the Minimalist Look, Anyway?

It's in, it's out, it's in again: Fashion trends make us crazy. The only fashion trend that's always in, as far as I'm concerned, is the minimalist look. Call it simple. Call it fundamental. The plain truth is that an unpretentious, unadorned, unembellished look—which is all minimalist really is—will *always* be one version of big city style, and will be lovely and right everywhere. You can't go wrong in chic, sleek minimalism: That means if you're transported to Washington from L.A., a gray monochromatic pantsuit will always look better at the embassy party than the Lilly Pulitzer floor-length red and pink floral skirt. Even if you were transported to Dallas, where the Pulitzer would be terrific, if you weren't sure about the floral, you could still draw more admiring glances in the gray pantsuit.

Bottom line: When in doubt, go minimalist. That could mean:

• A no-frills snug black wool sleeveless shell and matching slouchy pants.

•Mannish, low-slung trousers worn with a simple T.

•A gray suede camisole with black wool pants.

•A quietly elegant, long, chocolate jersey gown.

Minimal is street-smart, a major Big City Look, no matter what year it is.

The Art of Layering

Some street-smart women are architects. They build that Big City Look as deliberately as though they were building an apartment house, floor by floor. Layer by layer, they use imagination to add sweaters, vests, great shirts, belts, jewelry, scarves—to a basic classic outfit. They layer two contrasting shirts—one tucked in and the outside one knotted loosely. They layer strands of pearls with golden chains. They layer scarves over jackets. Layering works for style, it works for warmth, and it works for variety. You can shed or add layers as you move through your day or evening. For example:

You wear the stunning navy pinstripe suit to the office with a crisp white blouse and a boat-neck gray cashmere pullover over the blouse. Over one shoulder of the suit is slung an oversize red paisley shawl.

Now it's six P.M. You've got a dinner date with a business associate and want to dress up your look, just a little bit. Lose the blouse and scarf—they go into your desk drawer till tomorrow—and now the gray cashmere sweater alone peeks out from the suit jacket on which you've pinned a huge, silver brooch—a splendid look for that cocktail and dinner date.

Later, it's time for the theater with your lover. Off comes the sweater, to be stowed in your handy but stunning tote (no shopping bags, please). Now, under the suit jacket—*nothing*, only a little sensual décolleté. You switch the silver pin for diamond earrings. Perfect!

Shopping for Vintage Big City Style

Street smarts in fashion relies on unique touches. Shopping vintage almost always lends that unique touch that says you're hip enough to value the workmanship, impossible-to-duplicate fabrics, and individuality of the past. Many of my own clients are inspired by the best of long-gone decades. They find a twenties dress and a sixties hat in a vintage specialty store, loot their grandmothers' jewelry boxes for a turn-of-the-century brooch, and then, mixing and matching the antique touches with millennium style, they reinvent fashion.

Great buttons make a jacket.
Denise Hale knows it.

Overdosing on vintage looks silly. You need just the right, *restrained* touch if you're not to look as though you're going to a costume party. A fringed twenties dress, high button shoes, hat with feather, and that terrible fox scarf with the fox's face and little paws your grandma wore is not exactly subtle. When it works, though, vintage fashion is smashing and lends just that panache the woman with the Big City Look loves.

Last week everyone in the salon was coveting my client's picturesque, very Deco forties men's tie, which she wore with a classic white shirt. Another client was married in a magnificent white Victorian nightdress with the most exquisite lace I'd ever seen. The stars often opt for vintage. Demi Moore wore a forties lavender-gray halter gown to the 1992 Academy Awards, and Winona Ryder wore a fifties white bead and fringe dress for the 1994 Academy Awards. Stars like Courtney Love, Diane Keaton, Faye Dunaway, Lisa Kudrow, and Jennifer Tilly are all aficionados of vintage.

TIP: Don't buy anything vintage if it has an odor, if it's going to cost a Lexus to alter, or if it shows signs of moth damage.

SPECIAL EFFECTS

Accessories are the show stoppers, the little unconventional touches that bring a sense of urban style and individuality to your look. They are really more than "accessories." They're the special effects that affect others. *Harper's Bazaar* once decreed that great accessories seem to call out, "Touch me, feel me, wear me, let me be the star." When you spot a woman with The Look, first you take in her whole aspect, but then your eye is drawn to the unexpected special effects—the jeweled green snake appliqued onto black velvet gloves, the red leather cowboy boots, her fragrance, the texture of the unfinished edges of an exquisite linen scarf.

Special effects give you importance and style. They are integral to The Look. But here's a special tip: Never wear more than three or four accessories at one time. A scarf, a gold belt, and gold earrings are terrific. Add six gold buttons on the dress, and you look like a coin collection.

City Lights

Jewelry is city lights—flashes of gold and silver lending radiance to the persona as well as to face and fashion.

Try unusual antique jewelry.

- An antique sterling silver book or buckle on a chain.
- Vintage glass beads in floral colors.
- A turn-of-the-century portrait in a filigreed frame to be worn on a golden chain.
- Vintage gold men's cufflinks in the cuffs of a simple blouse or jacket.

Try ethnic jewelry. For an accessory that says *artistic*, opt for jewelry influenced by Asian, Indian, African, or other ethnic roots. They are one-of-a kind, sensual, and modern and ancient at the same time.

- Instead of the ubiquitous strand of white pearls, a double strand of French Polynesian black pearls or South Sea blue-gray pearls.
- A multistrand African beaded necklace.
- A tiny Moroccan silver purse hanging from a silver belt.

Try classic jewelry. When in doubt, it's always right.

- The classic, long, heavy, gold neck chain, in slim or wide versions, brings a flattering burnished glow to the face.
- Classic silver jewelry has an even more astonishing effect, particularly in ultrawide and chunky neck and wrist cuffs.
- Jet necklaces and brooches are also classic. Wear real jet, which is sparkling black and made from coal, not imitation jet, which cracks, scratches, and becomes dull.

Try earrings. Even if you've never worn earrings before, wear them! They *finish* a look like nothing else.

- Bold, big golden hoops or dangling modern designs.
- Superlarge silver geometrics.
- Square stone and metal combos.
- Diamond studs and rhinestone glitz.
- If you can only afford one great pair of earrings, make them pearls, which go with almost everything. I like smashingly large Mabe pearl earrings.

Try pins.

- Try big antique marquisite or stone brooches. Worn on a suit shoulder these look great.
- Ditto large silver or gold abstractions.

Left: Television personality Phyllis George in business mode. She's got The Look in a tailored white blouse, Ralph Lauren pantsuit, Renne Mancini pants boots, and Prada bag.

Above: Taking a meeting, Phyllis changes her look merely by changing her shirt and adding classic pearls and pearl earrings.

Right: Six hours later and ready to party, Phyllis changes her earrings and loses the blouse and the pearls. Dynamite. Layering works, as does reverse layering.

- Position the pin in a flattering and different place—high on a shoulder or low on the lapel, rather than in the traditional, over-the-heart spot.
- Good reproductions work as well as the real thing. Television star Jane Pauley is hardly ever seen without a wonderful pin—and it's almost always a reproduction.

Try watches. Technically, watches aren't jewelry, but don't you believe it. Besides grounding you in your time-frame, a great watch tells the world how savvy and serious you really are. Some options:

- The big-faced Swatch or the folksy Mickey Mouse watch.
- Stainless steel sport watches—you can't go wrong with Rolex or Omega.
- The Cartier tank with the leather strap—or a good knock-off—is absolutely classic.
- The dressier, dazzling versions encrusted with pavé diamonds or other precious stones.

City Scarves

Think of scarves as fabric jewelry, color catalysts that hold sophisticated outfits together. Scarves come in ingenious shapes and sizes, and for my money the bigger they are, the better! Oversize scarves are dynamite over a suit, coat, dress, or jacket. Do remember proportion, though. If you're very small, those oversize scarves can overwhelm your look. If you're very large, small scarves *under*whelm the Big City Look.

Four ways to wear a scarf: The over-the-shoulders fling.
The ascot. The tie. The loop.

The scarf should be compatible with or pick up the neutral color of your outfit: a navy suit, for example, might be splendid with an accent of a navy-red-yellow scarf over the shoulder. Also remember that a scarf doesn't have to be tied so *neatly:* the more expensive it is, the more it should appear as though you just looped it on casually—and it's *not* awfully elegant to tie it so the designer name or monogram is visible.

Here are my four favorite scarf looks:

The over-the-shoulder. Fling a long, oblong scarf (fringes at the ends are great) over one shoulder of a suit, dress, or coat so that it hangs down as far in the front as in the back. Position the scarf so that it casually drapes over the top of one sleeve.

Nina Griscom is a master at scarf tricks. Here's over-the-shoulder élan.

Nina in a wonderfully over-size navy and pink scarf that would lend The Look in any city.

The ascot. Tucked over or into the neckline of a dress or jacket (not too neat and perfect, please), the ascot lends instant verve!

The tie. A narrow scarf or even a man's tie, gently looped, is a woman's softer version of a man's knotted tie—and it looks simply lovely.

The loop. A wonderful oblong scarf, looped softly in a casual circlet around the neck, with both ends hanging down—the most delightfully sophisticated touch.

City Belts

Unexpected belts—a lemon-colored linen sash tying a body-skimming white jersey dress, a narrow golden chain belt hanging low on a black wool skirt, scarves encircling the waist—are all delicious, whether you're wearing a dress, pants, or skirt.

Leather belts, like all leather fashion, should only be made of the most supple, the most elegant leather. Patterned leather classics such as lizard or crocodile are always wonderful—the real McCoy *or* the fake. Metal buckles should not be tarnished or tacky; small buckles go best with narrow belts, and big, flashy buckles are great on simple pants and skirts. One of my clients has a stunning, wide sterling silver belt she bought in Morocco for a fraction of the cost she'd pay here. Studded with emeraldlike stones, slung low on even the simplest little black dress, it makes for a knockout look!

City belts: a wide leather belt with a classically simple silver buckle. Finish the look with a large silver bangle. Very Chicago, New York, and Washington, D.C.

City Hats

For an instant dose of city pizzazz, try a fabulous hat. Hats are in—even when they're out. Aside from warmth, they lend drama, intrigue, status. Don't let hats throw you. If the brim looks like it belongs down, flip it up anyway—to see what suits you. In the department-store hat department, try a fedora, a big-brimmed felt, a beret. Stick a pretty pin in it. Try them all. When you find a shape you love, adopt it in various permutations: straw or cotton in the summer, wool, felt, mohair in the winter.

A great hat can define the Big City Look—especially if it's a wide-brimmed maroon straw and especially if *USA Today* columnist Jeannie Williams is wearing it. Add a rakishly colorful scarf, and you're at home in any metropolis.

FINALLY . . . THE TEN COMMANDMENTS OF BAD TASTE

- Thou shalt not be slovenly. Torn is sometimes okay (e.g., the knees of some preworn Levi's). Stained is never okay.
- Thou shalt not be trendy. The peasant girl look was never big city. Neither were vinyl boots.
- Thou shalt not wear clingy, hanging-hem, missing-button, too-tight garments.
- Thou shalt not be a fashion victim. Matching everything is a major fashion sin of fashion victims.
- Thou shalt avoid the beast-of-burden look: Carrying several shopping bags is not tasteful, even if they match.
- Thou shalt avoid the mother-of-the-bride color. It's aqua. Avoid it even if thou art the mother of the bride.
- Thou shalt not wear run-down or poorly made shoes or purses.
- Thou shalt not roll up the waistband of thy pants or skirt. We'll know if thou do.
- Thou shalt not overdo things. Too much is worse than not enough, and this includes too much color, shine, texture, jewelry, or layering. A touch of outrageous is very different from too much.
- Thou shalt not wear itchy, scratchy, Brillo-like fabrics. They are the enemy.

The Bride
After every fashion show, it's customary to reveal—the bride! If you're to be a bride, plan ahead. Here's gorgeous Donna McPherson, looking for the right gown, getting transformed, and voilà— the prettiest bride in the world (as is EVERY bride in big and small cities anywhere). Wedding gown by Ulla Maija.

LANDMARK LOOKS:

Each of the big cities and their surrounding regions in our country has fashion landmarks that are as recognizable to the savvy as the Statue of Liberty is to tourists in New York. Here's what you might look like if you have the Landmark Look in any of the following cities.

Right: Rose Marie Bravo, CEO of Burberry's International, just radiates the New York landmark look . . . cultivated, cosmopolitan, and ready for the biting cold.

Center: Beth Decluitt in a rich-looking tomato-red St. John suit with gold braid trim at her home overlooking downtown Dallas.

Bottom: Claire Shipman, NBC's Washington correspondent, typifies the no-nonsense Big City Look. In her understated Ralph Lauren Power suit, she's stunning but ready for business. About her makeup: she has lots on—but you wouldn't know it, so subtle is the application.

Left: The irresistible Natalie Cole at home with an irre-sistible puppy. She has L.A. style to spare.

Center: Nicole Maserantonio in her raspberry-sherbet Christian Lacroix suit is ready for the club, the tea dance, or the business meeting. The Southern woman is pretty and powerful and always femi-nine.

Bottom: Kate Moore has the perfect Chicago Big City Look in her periwinkle-blue plaid Valentino jacket.

CHAPTER THREE
FACE

My client sits in my chair.

Her hair looks wonderful—sure it does, I just cut it. She's wearing a new Valentino and stunning, hip-high boots. By all rights she ought to be grinning and sitting tall, but she slumps, and she looks at herself sideways in the mirror, not straight on.

I start. Softly, softly I apply her makeup. *Soft* makeup. Gentle colors. Little by little, she sits taller.

And then she does it: *She sucks in her cheeks.* I've never put makeup on a client that didn't make her feel prettier and cause her, as if by reflex, to draw in those cheeks like a model.

Diane Sawyer has that universal Big City Look in every city in any country in the world. With her strikingly perfect oval face, champagne locks, and full, sensual mouth, anything she puts on looks chic. And take it from me: She has a gentle heart and a soul even more lovely than her face.

My client likes her face a lot. So do I.

It doesn't take a brain surgeon to know there's no such thing as one standard of beauty: Every face in the world is unique. And I respect the *natural* female face perhaps more than any other man alive. Having said that, let me also say this: Almost every face in the world—with or without perfect features—can use a little help, and as we approach the millennium, the vast array of available skin-care and beauty products and tools on the market is mind-boggling. The woman with the Big City Look takes advantage of them.

Let me help you put your best face forward.

WE'RE NOT ALL THE SAME

Even if the media and the magazines push us toward being a homogeneous country that eats the same foods, sees the same movies, and reads the same books, there are subtle regional differences in types of face care and color, just as there are in hair and fashion. Research tells us that the skin-care products and makeup we use often depend on where we live. What plays in Washington doesn't do it for Dallas. Every region has its own favorites and special needs.

If you live in Atlanta, you're going to have to pay more attention to sun blocks because that hot Georgian sun is murder. If you live in Washington, you'll need to deal more with the drying effects of steam heat and the abrasive effects of cold in the winter.

Let's consider some of those regional differences that exist in the way we like our faces to look.

THE CITY CODES: BEAUTY

Cracking the Southern Code: The Atlantan Face

Atlantans like their faces to register soft and easy. Call it a magnolia makeup: The Atlanta face is soft, soft, soft—peaches and cream when the skin is fair, coffee and cream when the skin is darker.

Evelyn Lauder, senior corporate vice president of Estée Lauder, Inc., says that young Atlanta women start using makeup earlier and younger than in most other regions. Southern women are most likely to be devoted to a certain brand of makeup, usually a brand of mascara or face powder. In fact, Southern belles wear more mascara and powder than women anywhere else. No wonder Clinique's Rinse-Off Eye Makeup Solvent is the line's bestselling skin-care product in Atlanta, and Clinique's Stay-Matte Pressed Powder is the bestselling makeup product.

Foundations are usually sheer, providing lighter coverage than the fuller coverage found in colder climates. The humid climate dictates that Atlantans don't have to worry too much about moisturizing their skin: Instead of using a separate moisturizer, they often opt for a lighter, lotion-based foundation that contains sunscreen. The most popular Estée Lauder foundation sold here is Enlighten. Chanel's Teint Naturel Liquid Makeup is an Atlantan crowd pleaser.

The color trends in Atlanta are growing less conservative and tend more toward pink than brown. The top-selling shade is Prescriptives' powder cheek color in Rose Dust and the line's Extraordinary Lipstick in a shade known as Mystery (a ruddy rose). Clinique's bestselling lip color is the Grapevine Chubby Stick, a cute, fat pencil perfect for the parching hot sun and the Atlantan theme of genteel and ladylike.

Finally, here's a secret southern tip I've heard from more than one Atlantan, not one of whom would be named because the idea isn't exactly genteel and ladylike. For those who sweat—and Atlantans don't even like the *word*—a light layer of Arrid Extra Dry antiperspirant sprayed on the face before applying makeup works wonders (close your eyes before spraying).

Cracking the Midwest Code: The Chicago Face

In down-to-earth, midwestern Chicago, blue or metallic eye colors are a hard sell, but Clinique does a fabulous business in Bronze Gel for polished, professional women trying to combat the consequences of frosty winters. The stores can't keep Bobbi Brown's Bronzing Powder on the shelves. Exfoliants, which slough off dead skin cells, also sell briskly here, especially Laszlo's Sea Mud granular soap bar. Turnaround Cream is Clinique's lead skin-care product, and Origins offers small tubes of hand-hydrating cream called Handle with Care, popular because the tubes can be easily toted in handbags. When it gets really cold, Chicagoans—and New Yorkers—often switch from a lotion to a cream moisturizer, which offers greater protection.

Origins balm, Rough Skin Soother, containing essence of St. John's Wort (newly popular from media exposure), sells well.

Chicagoans and their neighbors in the Midwest are the most conservative of all when it comes to color. They approach makeup much the way they build their wardrobes: sticking to classics and neutrals on their faces, as they do in their fashions. Every now and then they break out with an exciting touch of color for a dash of interest. Shiny red nail lacquers certainly do lend authority to power suits, but more often lipsticks and eye shadows are in rose or brown tones. Chicago women with The Look prefer foundations with fuller rather than sheer coverage, which have moisturizing benefits built in to protect their skin during the brutally cold winter months. Shiseido products sell well, as does the less costly Max Factor line.

Cracking the Mid-Atlantic Code: The Washington, D.C., Face

In conservative Washington and its environs, women buy more nail polish in neutral, classic beiges than anywhere else in the country. Ironically, sunscreens with lower SPFs (sun protection factor) sell better here than anywhere else in the country, though D.C. women are very focused on perfect skin.

Generally speaking, there's a new, overall American makeup trend, says Nikki Gersten, a spokesperson for Estée Lauder's Prescriptives line. "Color is back. The totally neutral face of the eighties has given way to the use of real color on the face for the next decade. And this applies to even the most conservative and business-oriented women in Washington, D.C., who is starting to change her makeup to express her moods on any given day or evening."

In face color, medium-tone shades—the earth browns, the gentlest reds—rather than very pale or very strong tones reign now in Washington. The three top-selling shades of lipstick are rosy-brown, soft cocoa, and a red-brick brown. Washingtonians generally use a complete makeup, one that always includes foundation, and they like full coverage in their foundations. Bobbi Brown's Foundation Stick in "Honey" sells fabulously in this part of the country. It's a lighter, subtler version of the old Max Factor Pan-Stik. Even when the makeup is heavy, it looks minimal because D.C. women are extraordinarily careful not to look overdone. Their business images must take priority. But just watch them at the D.C. balls, when glamour breaks out and long gloves are everywhere.

Washingtonians love a great moisturizer to counteract the effects of the cold, and Revlon's Eterna '27 All-Day Moisturizer is a top seller here. Origins puts out a popular product called Mint Wash, which provides cool cleansing for the hot and humid dog days of a Washington summer.

Even in understated D.C., even in the White House, a little blusher can't hurt. Vincent and Claire Shipman, NBC correspondent.

Cracking the Western Code: The Los Angeles Face

Los Angeles is the place where women experiment most with color and the place where women first pick up on new color trends, says Cheryl Crispin, vice president of communications at Estée Lauder. In L.A. you're most likely to see makeup used almost like a costume, to create a character. Here is where you'll note the silver-screen influences on makeup: the *Evita* look (fire-engine-red lips and a matte face), the *Flashdance* pale lips and heavy eyes of the eighties, and the Jane Austen–inspired dewy faces. L.A. women like to play! And if anyone can pull off the trendy lavenders, lilacs, and corals that appear every now and then, it's that L.A. woman—who ends up looking gorgeously natural anyway. The trick to displaying such vividness without seeming garish is to tone down color everywhere else. The woman with lavender lips is wearing a muted brown velvet jacket—not lavender to match. Also, I might add, she's very young. If you're a woman of a certain age, try lavender lips—and forget The Look.

Although L.A. women love the glamorously deep pink and red lips of the stars for evening, the bestselling shade here is softer, rosier. They also love to look year-round tan and healthy and a briskly selling sunless-tanning product is Origins Summer Vacation. Prescriptives' most popular cheek color is Soft Sun—a pinky-tan blush of color.

Women use more skin creams and lotions in L.A. and other points west than anywhere else in the country. The product of choice is Clinique's City Block SPF 15 sunscreen. I also love La Prairie's Essential Purifying Gel, used with a Buf-Puf. And Dermik Shepherd's Cream Lotion is an excellent unscented, inexpensive moisturizer that most good drugstores carry.

Don't miss L.A. fingernails. They're almost always short and pink or mauve—the better to play tennis and show off those tans. Finally, in L.A. attention must be paid to pretty feet peeking through the ubiquitous sandals. Origins Sole Searcher is a marvelously rejuvenating foot cream.

Cracking the Eastern Code: The New York Face

New York is edgy and sophisticated, with a lot of fresh-looking neutral face colors and a more stark, pale-perfect-porcelain aesthetic than, say, Atlanta or Chicago. A New Yorker may, one weekend, keep her lips pale, possibly even pearly, while she emphasizes her eyes with a smoky kohl look. Heavy sellers are Prescriptives' wonderful Softlining Pencil in Jet Black, which comes with a soft tip for smoky-smudging a hard line, and Cover Girl's Smoke Gray liner.

Then, being a New Yorker, on the next weekend, she'll do the exact opposite with a dark burgundy or brown mouth and very soft, neutral eyes.

Generally speaking, earthy cocoa shades of lipstick as well as "barely there" color are the hottest colors in New York, and Clinique's Black Honey Almost Lipstick sells well. New Yorkers also love Chanel's expensive but creamy lipsticks. Contrasting with "barely there" color are dark, garnet nail colors that practically fly off the shelves.

Let's talk contour. New Yorkers are experts at digging out bones where none existed before, and my very favorite contour powder is Diane von Furstenberg's Shader No. 10. Bobbi Brown also puts out a wonderful product, Bronzing Powder, Dark, that I use as a contour powder.

In the East, women are very savvy about sun and cold protection: They often use moisturizers with sun blocks and foundations with sun and wind protection as well, and the Lauder cream products always stand out.

Cracking the Southwest Code: The Dallas Face

In Dallas and its surrounding areas, women favor richly red lipsticks (a bestseller is Prescriptives' Extraordinary Lipstick in Red 1952). Dallas also loves bold, long, reddish-pink nails. You may have noticed—there's nothing shy about Dallas.

Probably because of the warm climate, women in Dallas like the matte look and hate shiny noses. They tend to use pressed powder all through the day and they love Prescriptives' Virtual Skin Pressed Powder. Chanel pressed powder comes in many colors and is also divine. There's nothing like Johnson's Baby Powder for loose powder.

In Dallas, the woman with The Look has a more fully made up face than she does in other parts of the country—not overdone, just carefully made up. She uses a foundation with good coverage—often Max Factor's Panstick—powder, eye shadow (the Clinique shadows are top-rate), blusher (Clinique's On Stage Mocha for brunettes or blondes sells well in Dallas), eyeliner, lipstick, and, always, lip gloss. Bobbi Brown's glosses are popular, as are the less costly Maybelline tinted glosses. Moisturizers help fend off the dryness of Dallas's hot afternoons, and in addition to the commercial brands I discuss in the skin-care section, I love those Evian-water purse sprays!

Nothing is left out on the Dallas face and nothing is left to chance. The overall effect is stunning—if not exactly natural. No wonder that bestsellers in Dallas are cleansing products. Mac puts out excellent products and Origins Sensory Therapy bath products with names like True Grit and Skin Diver are increasingly popular.

THE UNIVERSAL STANDARD

Despite regional differences, there is a universal standard—particularly in the appearance of the face. Certainly, as we've said, there are differences in preferences for color and care products. Pink lipstick doesn't seem to hack it in New York at all, while in Atlanta, it works wonderfully on the courts and on the courses. If you live in Washington, D.C., where the business ethic requires low-tone color on the face, you hunt out the brick-like, earthy tones in the makeup department and give short shrift to flaming reds; and Chicago women do the same. If you live in L.A., you tend to opt for lighter and even more vivid colors: The warmth of the landscape and the influence of Hollywood practically demand a less serious look. And rich Dallas demands rich hues—the bright, deep reds, for example.

Having said that, let me also state that deep down, I really believe that if the face looks terrific, it looks terrific anywhere. That's what I mean by the universal standard. For this standard, a subtle hand is what's *most* required: Makeup, no matter the color, should never look as if it's been applied with a trowel. I've noticed that women in D.C. probably wear more makeup than women in many other parts of the country, but it's applied so brilliantly, you're not aware of it.

I know that excellent, basic skin care is also universally effective. It works for everyone. What's good for your skin—keeping it clean and moist—is good for the skin of your best friend who lives a thousand miles away. The two of you just handle it differently. If you live in a hot climate where it's more difficult to keep the sun from your skin, you pay more attention to sun blocks. If you live in a place where the winds howl and the cold bites, you pay more attention to protective barriers and moisturizers on your skin.

Smoking is universally terrible. Nicotine restricts blood vessels and thus restricts circulation to the skin—as well as general circulation. Coffee is also universally damaging because caffeine has a very drying effect on skin—so stick with decaf if you must have coffee, no matter where you live.

Eating wisely is universally good. A diet high in the fluid content found in food like lettuce, citrus, cucumbers, fruits, leafy green vegetables, and melons moisturizes skin from the inside out, for everyone.

Finally, the universal standard of good taste—that true Big City Look—holds everywhere. Rough, raw patches on the skin are never appealing. Blatant, vulgar colors are never sophisticated. Foundation you can scrape off with a knife is never pretty.

The Big City Look means clean, healthy, radiant skin and gentle, apppealing makeup, *wherever* you call home.

The Choicest Products:
A Word of Advice

Don't put crummy products on your face. The best products don't necessarily cost the most money. My clients know that I value certain simple products like baby oil and Nivea Cream, avaliable in any drugstore. Still, many fine products *are* costly. So what! If you've tried them and they work for you, save up and buy them. I'd rather have you buy only one expensive but fine, pure cleanser or only one pricey but good foundation color than a dozen cheap products filled with substances that irritate the skin; the latter include fragrances, alcohol, oils, starchy fillers—even medication.

The Healthy Face:
Before the Paint, the Clean Canvas

Let's get started on universally wonderful skin care and makeup application. Before we consider makeup, the skin must be brought to its optimum, glowing condition: Without the proper skin care, no makeup in the world will be wonderful. Don't blame outside forces for skin eruptions. Chocolate does not give you pimples and neither do French fries; dirt and impacted oil glands give you pimples. If you don't clean the skin properly, you will have skin eruptions. And even if heredity has bestowed on you bags, sags, and postpuberty blemishes, you can still make the most of what you have by keeping your skin clean, moist, and well fed.

THE VINCENT
SKIN-CARE SYSTEM

Let this be your motto:

I Have to Clean, Wet, and Feed My Skin.

How to Clean Your Skin

Everyone needs to clean her skin thoroughly. Depending on the type of skin you have, there are small differences in approach.

Decide first what kind of skin you have—oily, dry, or combination. Here's how you can tell:

If your skin is dry:
- You often have chapped lips and flaky, alligator skin.
- Your face itches.
- Perhaps you have tiny, premature wrinkles around the eyes.
- Your pores are almost invisible.
- You sunburn easily and you're probably more fair than dark.
- You hate the broken capillaries around your nose.

If your skin is oily:
- Your nose glistens.
- Your hair is oily.
- Your face breaks out too often with blemishes or blackheads.
- You have enlarged pores.
- You're probably olive or sallow in complexion.
- Your skin does not hold makeup for very long: it congeals, blotches, or disappears in about an hour or so.

If you have combination skin:
- You have a dry area around the eyes or an oily area in the center of the face—one or the other and sometimes both.
- Your makeup doesn't congeal or blotch after an hour.
- You hardly ever get blemishes or dandruff.
- Basically, you tend to forget about your skin—it's pretty good and you take it for granted. This is the most common kind of skin.

CLEANING R$_X$ FOR DRY SKIN

Soaps are drying, and the more alkaline they are, the more they damage the skin's protective substances. I prefer an aloe cleansing cream, and there are many on the market. You might try St. Ives Aloe Vera Therapy Lotion or Vaseline Intensive Care Aloe Vera Lotion put out by Chesebrough-Ponds to remove dirt and makeup. Neutrogena's Fresh Foaming Cleanser is another gentle product, and Chattem Laboratories' Mudd Super Cleansing Treatment is good. Many of my clients with dry skin use pure mayonnaise as a natural cleanser, which they remove with tepid water. If you want to use soap, find a pure low-alkaline Castile soap like Dove. You may choose to exfoliate your skin—remove the dead cells that sit on the surface using cream or light massage—but dry skin owners must use an especially gentle approach because dry skin is more easily damaged than oily and broken capillaries are never pretty.

CLEANING R$_X$ FOR OILY SKIN

What makes your skin oily are sebaceous glands that overproduce. The good news is that oily skin looks more supple and younger longer. The bad news is that you have a tendency to get acne and your nose and forehead shine. You need efficient, deep-cleansing routines and an effective but not harsh cleansing agent especially formulated for oily skin. Your pharmacist can help you choose one, or you might try a soap with no detergents like Neutrogena soap for normal to oily skin, Neutrogena for skin with acne, or Neutrogena's Transparent Facial Bar made with glycerine. Many of my clients use a mixture of simple witch hazel mixed with a few drops of lime juice to clean.

Three or four times weekly, after washing the face, you might also use a gentle, nonabrasive exfoliant like Buf-Puf or Lancôme's Bienfait Démaquillant, cleansers that remove the dead skin flakes that block pores. The top layer of skin that's visible is called the epidermis; it replaces itself every twenty-eight days as the dead skin cells flake off. Cleaning off the flakes minimizes pore size and allows moisture to penetrate more deeply. Gently massage the scrub onto clean, wet, soaped facial skin, avoiding the delicate tissues surrounding the eye area. After exfoliating, dab a gentle, low-alcohol astringent on the skin to help remove oil and traces of the cleanser. I recommend Almay's Counter Balance Pore Lotion, Lancôme's Tonique Douceur, or even simple Dickinson's Witch Hazel. Many astringents are prepared with antibacterial agents that are also useful for combating blemishes. Rinse with clean water. Simple.

CLEANING R$_X$ FOR MATURING SKIN

If you're a "woman of a certain age," try Elizabeth Arden's Millenium Hydrating Cleanser. It floats away grime. Really.

How to Moisturize (or Wet) Your Skin

MOISTURIZING R$_X$ FOR DRY SKIN

Americans spend a fortune every year on placenta creams, ointments, emollients, cocoa butter, coconut oil, beeswax, avocado cream, and other forms of exotica that promise to moisturize your face. Most of these products can't help the layer of cells we know as skin. Claims that they "nourish" the skin are plain silly. The outer layer of skin is dead and can't be fed or nourished from the outside.

Dry skin lacks water moisture, not oil. The skin needs you to supply moisture to the skin in the form of water, then trap that moisture on the skin to prevent it from evaporating. There are many good products on the market that do just that—Clinique products are wonderful for sealing in moisture (try Turnaround Cream), and so is a product called Redken pH Plus Moisturizing Skin Balancer (particularly when used at night). Estée Lauder's Advanced Night Repair is also a fine moisture sealant. One of the finest products on the market is Elizabeth Arden's Ceramide Time Complex Moisture Cream. Applying an inexpensive petroleum jelly, baby oil, or a simple product like Nivea Cream to the skin right after bathing, when the skin is moist with water, also works well.

Frankly, the *best* way to moisturize dry skin is from the inside out, and the best product in the world to do that with is water in many applications. Drink at least seven to eight glasses of water daily; the bloodstream will carry it through the body and the moisture will infiltrate the skin.

TRICKS THE MODELS USE: OTHER WAYS TO MOISTURIZE WITH WATER

- Use warm, not hot, water in your bath or shower: Hot water opens pores and increases moisture loss.
- Lower the heat at night. Put pans of water on the radiator to raise humidity.
- Try sleeping with a vaporizer on in the bedroom.
- Spray mineral water on your face. Purse-sized spray bottles are available everywhere (those Evian atomizers!).

MOISTURIZING R$_X$ FOR OILY SKIN

After cleaning and rinsing your skin, seal in some of the last rinse water with a moisturizer. I recommend Shiseido Moisturizing Lotion or Oil of Olay Moisture Replenishing Cream as effective seals if not really moisture providers. All skins—oily ones as well as dry—need moisturizing, so faithfully drinking those seven to eight glasses of water daily is a must for you. Diet counts, too, enormously. We feed the skin from the inside out with proper nutrition.

Aerobic exercise is an excellent way to moisturize any type of skin and it seems to work wonders, especially with more oily skins. Exercise stimulates circulation and sweating and thus brings the body's moisture to the skin's surface. Improved blood circulation derived from aerobic exercise feeds the skin and makes it glow. Good blood circulation also stimulates oil glands so they don't clog and produce blemishes.

CLEANING AND MOISTURIZING R$_X$ FOR COMBINATION SKIN

Avoid products with heavy fragrance or alcohol. Moisturize often (see tips for dry skin) from the inside to the outside. If you have an oily T-shaped area around and under the nose, pat just that area with a light astringent before you go to bed. On dampened skin, apply petroleum jelly or baby oil around the eyes and lip areas only. When you wake up, clean with Origins gentle Liquid Crystal or another nonalkaline cleanser. Spray water on your face from your portable mineral water spray, as many times a day as you remember to do so. Listen to your skin: If it feels taut and dry, moisturize in those dry areas only.

Please stay out of the sun. This means everyone—even you with the olive or black skin! The dermatologists are not feeding us hype. They mean it: Sun is big trouble and is the culprit behind most skin cancer and premature aging. If you can't stay out of the sun, use a sun-block cream with an SPF of at least 15. And learn to love wide-brimmed hats.

THE VINCENT MAKEUP: THE INSIDE TRACK ON WHAT YOU NEED AND HOW TO USE IT

Before we begin, just as you emptied your closet for the shopping expedition, empty out your makeup cabinet, using these guidelines:

- If you haven't used it in six months—OUT!
- If you can't identify it—OUT!
- If the covers or tube tops are missing—OUT!
- If it smells funny—OUT!
- If it came with a gift-with-purchase and is a garish or "not-you" color—OUT!
- If the brushes are ancient or clotted or hard—OUT!

The Vincent makeup:
Foundation gives an even palette.
Contour is brushed in the hollow under the cheekbones (and brushed down the side of a wide nose for narrowing).
Blusher is powdered on the cheekbones.
Powder sets the whole thing.
Lashes are curled and mascaraed, liner and shadow are applied as described.
Lip liner is blended into lip color.

About brushes. All you need are three good, fat sable brushes: a small one for eye shadow, one for contour, one for powder and blusher. Good brushes can be cleaned in the top tray of your dishwasher, but don't put them through the drying cycle.

Make sure you have a mounted magnifying mirror where you make up—even if your vision is perfect! And try to place it in natural light.

The Canvas

Every makeup artist has a favorite order to making up. Here are the steps for a beautiful makeup via the Vincent approach.

THE FOUNDATION

Always begin with the foundation. I always tell my clients to opt for water-based foundations applied with a damp sponge, no matter what type of skin they have. These foundations give the best coverage as well as a radiant, dewy look. I love Elizabeth Arden's Flawless Finish Everyday Makeup SPF10. For serious coverage, some of my clients also like the old-fashioned Max Factor Pan-Stik, applied with a wet sponge to cut the thickness.

The Foundation's Color

Every department store offers what seems like millions of foundation colors to paint the canvas of your face. But the foundation's job is not so much to change the color of your natural skin as to *even out* the myriad colors in your natural skin and provide a consistent canvas for your portrait. I like an opaque foundation base in one of just three or four beigy shades—no matter your skin color. Dark shades do not provide better coverage. They only serve to stain blemishes and make them more obvious. About the color of your foundation:

- Pale skin takes a very pale beige shade.
- Olive skin takes a pink-beige shade that cuts through the yellows in the olive.
- Ruddy skin takes a true beige shade—no pink tones.
- Black skin takes a deep shade of beige.

This is the rule that should govern your foundation's color: The shade you choose should be a drop lighter than your own complexion. Where is it written that you have to stick to the foundation shades you're offered by manufacturers? Experiment by mixing and matching. Blend colors on the back of your hand to find the right shade for you. When you find a terrific foundation shade, just right for this week, anyway—pour the mix into a fresh bottle, and you have your own, personalized foundation. Your skin changes color periodically (with sun exposure, for example), so it's good to have a couple of foundation colors and textures in your makeup cabinet.

Applying the Foundation

With liquid foundations, take a slightly dampened sponge, apply some foundation color to the sponge, and paint your face (including lips), under your face, and your neck for complete coverage. The look should be even, not chalky or spotty. A prepared and uniform canvas.

THE CONCEALER

The next product in your arsenal to be applied is the concealer, a thicker, opaque product that does its best to hide dark lines, circles, shadows under eyes, pimples, veins on eyelids, burst blood vessels around the nose, and other enemies. I often use Elizabeth Arden's Perfect Covering Concealer. Choose a shade lighter—*not* darker—than your foundation. Sometimes, for large areas, I begin with a touch of a green-tinted concealing cream known as a "neutralizer," which camouflages yellows, blacks, and grays in the skin. Then I use the concealer where needed over this cream.

After the foundation is applied, with your fingers or a dry sponge, dot the concealer on an offending area. Don't apply the concealer before the foundation, or the concealer will swim away as you begin to blend the foundation. Blend over the concealer with more foundation. For puffy eyes, dot the concealer on the line of demarcation *under* the puffiness; if you put the concealer on the whole puffy area, it will highlight, instead of conceal, the puff.

Blend, blend, blend. "Blend" is the most important word in this makeup chapter. If your foundation is not skillfully blended into the neck and under the chin, you'll look as though you're wearing a mask. If your concealer is spotted and not blended into the foundation, you'll look like a leopard. Blending marks the difference between a subtle makeup and an amateurish job. Of course, don't blend to the point where the blemish shows through again! The last step is to blend yet again with a puff or brush coated with a thin layer of translucent powder.

TIP: If you have to cover a major blemish—say, an ill-considered tattoo—get a medical concealer, one especially created to cover birthmarks, scars, etc. Covermark puts out a good one. Dot it on the offending mark, then blend over it with your regular foundation, dot again, blend again. Set with a pat of powder.

Dig out those bones with contour powder.

CONTOUR

Next, contour. Contour is the product that will magically dig out hollows under your cheekbones where none exist and emphasize those that you already own. Contouring powder or cream (I much prefer the powder) also highlights the structure of your face and makes double chins, wide noses, and sagging necks less obvious. Contour is a magical product applied after the concealer.

Contour should always be in a rich, rusty-brown shade—no pinks or reds, please! To reveal your cheekbones, use a good, flat-end sable brush to brush contour in the hollow *under* the cheekbones and blend outward from the middle of the cheek into the hairline in an upward slant. You just have to experiment with contour powder to get the best results. Try the following:

- Contour powder brushed down each side of a wide nose makes fleshy, fat areas seem to disappear—the nose narrows before your very eyes!
- Contour powder brushed along and just under the chin and jawline paints out neck sags and double chins—not as skillfully as a plastic surgeon, but it's the next best thing.
- Contour powder brushed on the tip of a nose along the nostrils in a V (for Vincent, of course!) narrows the end of the nose.
- Contour powder down the center of a hooked nose minimizes the hook.
- Don't go too nuts with contour. If you don't blend it properly, or if you overuse it, your face will look dirty.

THE BLUSHER

After the contour comes the color. Blusher can consist of powder—I love Elizabeth Arden's Cheek Color—and be powdered on the cheekbones. I also like a dot of cream rouge, skillfully blended *on* (not under) the cheekbones and out into the hairline. Blusher should be a gentle red or coral and always blended in so you can't tell exactly where the color ends and the rusty-brown contour begins. Dot and blend the smallest drop of blusher on your chin and forehead also—the natural blushing spots.

THE POWDER

A matte finish is far prettier than a shiny finish. Powder makes a matte finish, sets the makeup, and blends the color. It comes in a pressed compact or loose—choose your preference. Powder should rarely have color; it should be, in effect, translucent. There is one exception: Despite the no-color rule, sometimes I do use a soft, mauve shade of powder on olive complexions. Chanel puts out a great one.

I apply powder with a sable brush several times, between each application of foundation, contour, and blusher.

Two powder tips:

- In case of a cosmetic powder outtage, plain old baby powder does the trick.
- Light accentuates an area, dark makes it recede. If you softly powder in the corner of the eyes, then bring the powder down to a half-crescent under the eyes, then bring it down to both sides of the mouth, the result is a radiance that lends a flattering play of light to the face.

If you've laid on the makeup too thickly and don't feel like starting from scratch to tone it down, use a dampened natural sponge to blend the face to more subtle dimensions. Finally, after you've made up your face, set it with a spray of water from your purse-sized atomizer. Do your eyes next.

Makeup Tools:
Good brushes are magic; use them for blusher, contour, powder, lips, and eyelashes. Subtle colors are key. These Trish McEvoy products are wonderful.

The Most Beautiful Eyes in the World

If you happen to meet the eyes of the woman with the Big City Look, you'll see they're hauntingly beautiful. Here's all you need for hauntingly beautiful eyes:

One eyelash curler. I know that many women have thrown out their eyelash curlers, but I can't imagine why. Gently curled lashes lift the eyelids and open the eyes wider.

Four powder eye shadows. Chestnut brown, steel or charcoal gray, taupe (soft, not metallic), and bronze for evening. You could get away with two of these. Plus you need small applicators with foam tips to apply the shadow.

Three soft pencil eyelash liners. Charcoal, chestnut brown, a deeper sable.

Two tubes of mascara. Sable brown (use jet black only if your eyelashes are naturally jet black) and midnight blue (see the night-look tip below).

FIRST, THE CURLER

Use the curler before the color. Hold the clean lashes in the curler's opening as close to the eyelash line as possible and close it gently to make sure you've not captured any skin along with the lashes. When you're sure you can squeeze the eyelash curler shut tightly without catching any skin, and being careful not to change the position of the curler, give four to six hard little squeezes. If you release the lashes and go back to capture them again for another squeeze, disaster! Bent lashes.

SHADOW PLAY

Now, the lid color. With a small, spongy applicator or fluffy brush, brush a light-colored shadow—perhaps a quiet gray or a taupe—over the entire lid and up to meet the eyebrow. This is a highlighting color that will give space to the eye and make it seem more open. Since lightness brings an area forward, the width and the space of the eye will be exaggerated by this lighter color. *Never* use metallics or frosted shadows, which look cheap and accentuate wrinkles.

When this color is evenly blended, go back and apply a slightly darker version of the highlighting shadow over the lid, starting right above the lash line; then blend it into the highlighting color. Since darkness conceals, a puffy or drooping eyelid will be "painted away" with this darker color.

TIP: Eye shadow and liner colors should complement, not match, your eyes. For example, blue shadow and blue liner detract from blue eyes—in addition to being ugly!

The model Silke is wearing a lot of makeup—so subtly applied that it looks soft and natural. Note the shadow play on her lids and the cheek contour powder. In a classic Donna Karan little black dress with her hair gelled back, she's ready for work or play.

Delicately shade the darker-color shadow in the inner corner of the eye. Let the shadow line get smudgier and thicker as it flows to the outer corner of the eye and a *teeny* bit out beyond the corner. Blend so you can't tell where the highlight color stops and the lid color begins.

TIP: Slightly dampened cotton swabs (or try the marvelous Q-Tips Cosmetic Applicators) are your best friends for correcting mistakes.

TIP: Experiment by mixing and matching two colors—a soft brown and black, perhaps—to get a lovely shadow color that's perfectly right and perfectly unique.

NEXT, THE EYELINER

After the shadows comes the liner. The person who invented crayon eyeliner deserves the Medal of Honor. Eyes become luminous with this extraordinary product.

Some of my clients use an old-fashioned technique that also gives a nicely subtle result: They dip a soft, pointed brush in water, then in a charcoal or brown eye shadow powder. With this they paint on the eye line for a natural smudgy effect.

Whatever you use to line the eye, start the eye line one third of the way from the inner corner of the eye (starting at the inner corner makes the eyes appear too close together). Draw a subtle, soft line right along the lash line. There should never be a space between the lash line and the crayon line. Softly blend the line with the tips of your fingers or even a cotton swab. Don't let the crayon line extend beyond the lashes in wings—that went out with Cleopatra. For a finished look, put a bit of smoky eye shadow on a swab and trace over the line to soften it. Never apply color to the inside rim of your eye—the wet part. First, it usually disappears in two minutes. Second, it can easily injure the eye. Third, it often ends up a big, dark, wet mass in the corner of the eye—really attractive.

My signature V: When the shadow is complete, I usually add the softest, almost imperceptible V's (for Vincent) like pointed parentheses at the outer corner of the eyes: It enlarges and emphasizes.

NOW, THE MASCARA

Use the thickest dark brown mascara you can find. Apply two or three coats and let them dry in between. No clumps, please. A tiny comb (I like a metal one for this purpose) will get rid of excess mascara flakes as you go along. You want the mascara to last forever—or at least the evening? Lightly pow-

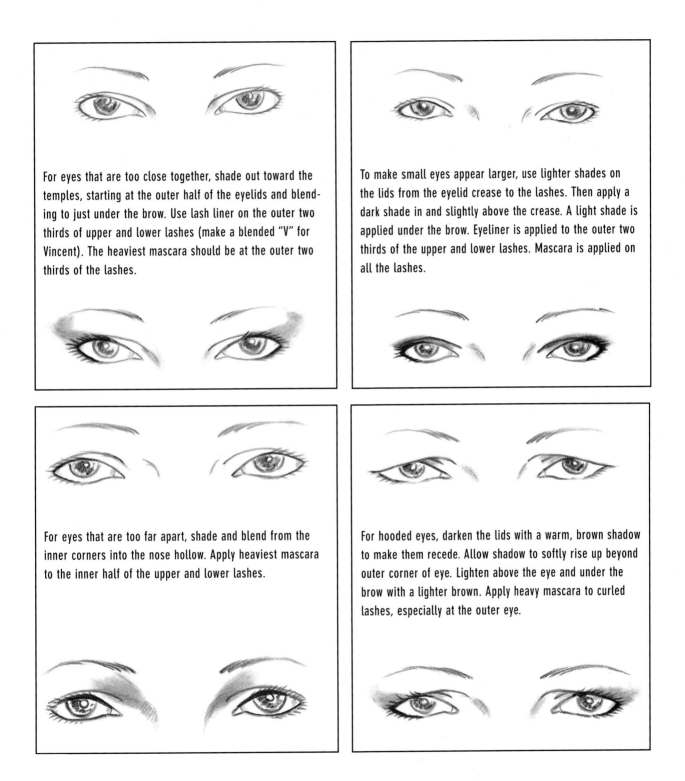

For eyes that are too close together, shade out toward the temples, starting at the outer half of the eyelids and blending to just under the brow. Use lash liner on the outer two thirds of upper and lower lashes (make a blended "V" for Vincent). The heaviest mascara should be at the outer two thirds of the lashes.

To make small eyes appear larger, use lighter shades on the lids from the eyelid crease to the lashes. Then apply a dark shade in and slightly above the crease. A light shade is applied under the brow. Eyeliner is applied to the outer two thirds of the upper and lower lashes. Mascara is applied on all the lashes.

For eyes that are too far apart, shade and blend from the inner corners into the nose hollow. Apply heaviest mascara to the inner half of the upper and lower lashes.

For hooded eyes, darken the lids with a warm, brown shadow to make them recede. Allow shadow to softly rise up beyond outer corner of eye. Lighten above the eye and under the brow with a lighter brown. Apply heavy mascara to curled lashes, especially at the outer eye.

der lashes in between coats.

For an absolutely smashing night look, put on your sable-colored mascara, then, *on the tips of the lashes only*, an application of midnight blue or navy. The eyes smolder suggestively. Bellissimo.

THE BROWS

And what of the brows? In my opinion, you ought to have your brows shaped professionally, at a good salon. I've seen too many disasters from overactive and undereducated tweezers. Once you've had your brows shaped professionally, you can keep the shape by just plucking away strays. You hate the pain of plucking? Do it after a shower when the warmth has loosened up the follicles and after you've applied some baby teething cream onto the brow area. An ice cube applied to the skin for a minute or so before the big pluck provides a natural anesthesia.

If you really feel you need to fill in your brows, use a nongreasy eyebrow pencil such as Prescriptives Softlining Pencil. For a more natural finish, take a small brow brush and rub it against the pencil point, then brush the fill-in color onto the brow with the brush instead of the pencil. If you must use a pencil directly on the brow, the idea is to fill in bare spots—not create new brow hairs—so apply the brow color with short, light-touch strokes. Less is always more.

Brush the brows up with a clean old toothbrush. Nothing more wonderfully opens the eyes. Spray a little hair spray on the brush to keep that brow in line.

What a Mouth!

I leave the lips for last because the mouth is the number one turn-on for men. From a Big City Look standpoint, if the mouth is wrong, it's all over.

Luscious lips are achieved by following:

- A lip-liner pencil in a natural burgundy or earth-brown color—the color of most lips.
- A tiny, soft-bristle brush.
- A beautiful shade of lipstick (beautiful is not fuchsia, is not dark brown, is not black).
- A pot of lip gloss.

Start by making sure the makeup foundation has been applied over the lips as well as the rest of the face, to prepare the mouth for uniform color. With a good sable brush, lightly dust the mouth with powder; this will set the color to come.

Carefully line your mouth with the lip-lining pencil. This line will eventually be blended into the lips; there is nothing more amateurish and less luscious then a finished mouth outlined with a telltale coloring-book line.

Defining Nina Griscom's sensual mouth with lip liner.

TIP: Don't try to make your lips really full if they're really narrow, or make them much smaller than they are. Excessive lip-shape changes always look terrible. You can make them just the barest millimeter fuller if they're narrow or a tiny bit more narrow if you feel they're too full.

With a tiny brush that's been dipped into the lipstick color, paint inside the outline, then blend this color into the line. You can experiment here nicely. Try using another color on top of the one you've just applied. Sometimes, experimentation comes up with the prettiest colors never yet sold.

Many clients apply the lip liner *after* they've applied lipstick, gently blending it into the mouth color; they say it's easier for them to define the lips.

If you admire a really sexy mouth, dip a small brush into a pot of clear lip gloss, or you can even use a gold-tinted gloss. Apply it lightly to just the center of the bottom lip. *Lightly.* Your mouth should not look like an ice-skating rink. Blend a little.

Here's another option: For some women, it's about *lips*, not *lipstick*. Ever see a stunning woman with The Look and she's wearing barely perceptible color on her mouth? Sometimes the slightest of color stains on the mouth rather than a more definitive color can be smashing. Your choice.

So there it is, the Vincent Makeup.

Lookin' good, big city woman, lookin' good!

WHAT MAKES THE BIG CITY LOOK?

Fashion, hair, and face are geography. They may wear more makeup in Dallas than they do in Chicago. They may wear more sun block in Atlanta than they do in Washington. They may wear more mascara in New York than in L.A. To wear makeup appropriate to your region is always a good idea. But remember: A clean, subtly made up face is at home everywhere.

MY FINAL ADVICE

If you've spent more than twenty minutes on your makeup, that's at least ten minutes too long.

CHAPTER FOUR
ATTITUDE

Now we get to it: attitude. This is what separates the ordinary woman from the extraordinary one, the uninteresting woman from the fascinating one, the simply pretty woman from the woman with the Big City Look. Attitude is the quality that shines from your face and posture, from your eyes, from your walk. Attitude makes you memorable.

The recent headline in the *New York Times* read,

Sullen Got Old. The Attitude Now Is Fabulous.

You bet it is.

ABC journalist Cynthia McFadden has attitude. Very Greta Garbo. Nothing like it for that Big City Look. Clothes by Calvin Klein.

In the last couple of decades, fashion, makeup, and fragrance marketers have tried to push grumpy, grungy, and sullen as the attitude to own. Perfumes were named Poison, Opium, Obsession. Angry-looking waif children with torn underwear were everywhere. Resentful faces were fashionable. The attitude we were supposed to emulate was doom and gloom.

The woman with the Big City Look never bought it. For her, the attitude always was *happy*.

Not then—and not now—would she try to affect a dreary, druggy, grungy attitude. Instead, her look is confident and happy—not the inane, yellow happy face of the seventies but the self-assured, optimistic happy of the coming millennium. The kind of happy that says, "Sure, we all have problems—but I can deal with them." The kind of happy that makes you want to follow her down the block, so appealing is her upbeat air.

It's wonderful when happy and confident go together, but listen: Even if you're not feeling particularly happy at any given moment, you can still feel confident. It's that air of confidence that ultimately makes or breaks the woman with The Look. Caring enough to get your look together, caring enough to get your body working and feeling right is a huge confidence booster. Trust me.

ATTITUDE HITS THE STREET

Just what is it that bestows the kind of seductive confidence you see radiating from the woman on the big city street in your town?

First of all, walk tall. Great posture and a firm stride are essentials of The Look. And never make a statement that sounds as if it has a question mark at the end ("Pass the butter, please?" "Don't put oil in my salad?" "I need to take Tuesday off?"). You need to walk boldly, powerfully, as though you have somewhere special to go; you need to speak with authority, as though everyone knows that what you say is important.

I believe that one needs three basic qualities to radiate vibes of inner self-reliance, confidence, and joy in just *being*. These qualities can be acquired if you practice.

- You need to be aware.
- You need to be unafraid of taking small risks.
- You need to feel good.

You Need to Be Aware

Let's start here. Self-confidence isn't grabbed from the air—it's learned. You need to be informed, aware of what's happening in this fascinating world, and confident that you *are* well informed. Just knowing you're savvy makes you walk with straighter shoulders, gives you *attitude*.

Read the newspaper daily, even if you disagree violently with the columnists. Any woman who's not aware of the larger world cannot feel confident in her smaller world. You don't need to solve the problems of Bosnia, but you do have to know that Bosnia exists. Read book reviews and

Texas born and bred, the fabulous Liz Smith has big city style no matter what she wears—in this case, zebra socks. Writing her column on a friend's lounge, Lizzie exudes a happy, confident attitude. (Photograph © Harry Benson of *Life*)

the bestseller list of your regional big city newspaper to have an idea of what people are reading. Books are good for the soul and the mind. They force you to think.

In short, *you have to have opinions*—yes, you do, if you're not to feel left out and slow-witted! In order to have opinions, you have to be informed so that you can keep up with conversations and allusions dropped by your boss, your friend, your colleagues, and not sound out of it. So decide now to read at least one newspaper every day, not to mention at least one weekly newsmagazine. Also watch the news on TV. In addition, try to browse through one or two women's *and* men's magazines regularly—those that deal with appearance, health, and issues—just to be on the cutting edge of what's new.

To be really aware, you should become an expert in something. Take a course in a subject you know nothing about—birdwatching? City architecture? Antiques? Self-confidence is easily bred when you know more than most others about a fascinating subject. What if no one ever talks about architecture in your circles? Don't worry—you'll always find ways to weave new knowledge into conversation once you own the knowledge. When you concentrate on a subject, you'll be amazed at how often it does crop up in life—even when it never did before. Suddenly, you'll read headlines about controversial city architecture, your friends will talk about buildings they hate, you'll be inundated with references to architecture. Being aware and very conversant on a particular subject makes you interesting.

You Need to Be Unafraid of Taking Small Risks

That means keeping an open mind—not being arrogant about what you already know to be true. To keep an open mind, you really have to get in the habit of testing what you know, taking small risks, and breaking the rules—not only the rules others have set for you but the ones you've set for yourself.

But notice that I said *small* risks. You don't have to risk your way of life, your look, and your job to exude an air of happy confidence. It's the small, calculated risks you should take—the ones that give you confidence if you turn out to be right but don't create disaster if you're wrong.

You can train yourself to take small chances in every part of your life. Why *not* visit an astrologer, just for the fun of it, even if you've never believed in astrology? Why *not* try the sushi or the wild boar, even if you've

Attitude à la Kelly Curtis. The girl with the Big City Look has it made in the shade.

never dreamed of tasting such exotica? Why *not* swim with the stingrays in the Cayman Islands instead of taking your usual Florida vacation? Saying yes to the small risks opens up your personality, says you're game to try new things, gives you an aura of *attitude*.

Here's an example of taking a small risk in something as simple as your dress code. Break the rules of fashion, such as "Wool in the winter"; "White in the summer"; "No glitz to the office." Suppose you live in a small town in Minnesota and your best friend makes fun of your favorite fashion magazine—"Will you look at what they're wearing in New York!" she says with a laugh. *"Sequins to the office!"* Secretly, you admire the look of the model she's pointing to. Of course, you wouldn't wear a skintight sequined dress to your work as the town attorney—but how about just a glimpse of a sequined or lacy camisole under your pinstripe power suit? Wouldn't that be fun? Wouldn't that bring admiring glances your way? Sure it would— and you wouldn't have to take a huge chance, break the rules in a major way. All you'd have to do is take a small risk. A glimpse of that camisole would be perfectly appropriate for your position, but it would still set you apart a bit, make you look different, like a risk taker who is confident of her appeal. Taking a small chance, even in fashion, sets you free in a big way. You can prove not only that white has a life beyond summer or that a little bit of glitz can go to the office, but also that you are a confident, free-spirited woman with attitude, with the Big City Look.

You Need to Feel Good

How can you even appear to have a fabulous attitude if you don't feel good, strong, and serene? Can't be done.

This is not a book about medical solutions, so I have to assume that if you don't feel just right, you're getting the best medical attention you can find. However, there are routes other than medical to an attitude of inner serenity and a body that works like a well-oiled machine and brings envious stares when it moves down the avenue.

People do different things to stay fit. At the traditional gyms in L.A. and New York, just about the only thing that's not negotiable is one's work-out. In Chicago, fitness is often pegged to a sporty passion for biking, hiking, or canoeing on one of Chicago's great lakes. In Dallas they say that women get as competitive at the gym as they do at beauty pageants. In Atlanta, fashion reigns on the courts, at the racecourses, and in the spas, and in Washington the gym is the supreme networking arena.

Working out is in, from the biggest cities to the smallest hamlets. Wherever you go in this great land, women are certainly working out their bodies, but women with the Big City Look and the greatest savvy also work out their spirits and their minds to bring vitality and peace into their lives.

ATTITUDE LIFTERS

Clients and friends all over the country always tell me about their favorite places (usually they're spas) and activities that help them unwind and get in touch with health and serenity. I call them *attitude lifters*. Hairstylists, as you know, are the fonts of all information. What follows are very brief descriptions of some attitude lifters—therapies that people whom I trust use to make themselves feel good. If you're interested in experimenting with a particular approach, call the national headquarters of that approach (listed here or in your own local phone book) for more information.

NOTE: Although the following alternative approaches have each been recommended by many knowledgeable clients, it's always a good idea to consult with your medical doctor before embarking on new programs.

But know this: The attitude you need if you're to have the Big City Look requires you to feel good. If you want to step out of your everyday doldrums and take a small chance on a new way of feeling good, think about trying out one of the following—and ask for prices before you commit.

SPAS

A great place to begin walking taller and feeling better is at a spa, and there are sure to be some wonderful ones in or near your area. A week, a weekend, or even a day at a local health spa will set you on the road to thinking differently about your body and about wellness in general. Many spas have lectures on nutrition and spirituality as well as marvelous body massage, exercise, and nutrition services.

There are spas and there are spas—spas for couples or just men or women, spas where a muscle-bound guy named Jorge pummels your back to total relaxation, spas where they give you a pink robe and one day costs as much as a vacation in Bermuda, spas where you luxuriate in mud or mineral water, spas where all you get are massages of one type or another, spas where they wrap you in a cocoon of steaming linen sheets that have been brewed in herbs, and spas where you mostly think. If you feel you've been even slightly neglectful of your body and your spirit, choose one that seems right for the transformation of your attitude. How to find a spa? Word of mouth is always the best way. Also, look at the many books on the subject available at bookstores and at the library. I especially like *Spa-Finders Guide to Spa Vacations*, by Jeffrey Joseph (John Wiley, 1990)and Fodor's *Healthy Escapes* (Fodor Travel Publications, 1996).

All the spas offer what I call attitude lifters—various practices that not only feel good but often make you look at life in a new, positive, assertive way.

You don't have to go to a spa to experience these, though the total environment at a spa may in itself be an attitude lifter. What follows are just a sampling of attitude lifters. How do you find out about them? Again, word of mouth leads you to attitude-enhancing therapies. Pay attention when a friend or colleague says, "You must try yoga—or reiki—or reflexology"—or whatever it is that has made her walk tall. The local Yellow Pages will also direct you to independent practitioners or institutes offering attitude-enhancing therapies. Here's a sampling of what's possible.

MASSAGE AND BODYWORK

Massage is the quintessential attitude lifter. It's just plain nice to be kneaded.

Swedish massage, the classic touch therapy, revs up circulation (which benefits both the nervous and muscular systems), cuts down fatigue, and produces the most pleasurable, sensuous, self-affirming haze around a body that a body can imagine. It's a healing art.

Do you think a Swedish massage would be a terrific attitude lifter—but you don't want to go to a spa, you don't even want to move from your bedroom, and you don't want to try the telephone book because you fear getting involved with some flaky, kinky service? You might try The Quiet Touch, a massage service that makes house calls (Goldie Hawn, Molly Ringwald, and the Trumps are steady customers). Dial 800-MASSAGE and ask for the prices for a rubdown in your own bedroom.

Shiatsu is a Japanese method of pressure massage following energy patterns, or "meridians," of the body. The practitioner applies pressure to points along the meridians to restore energy flow and promote healing. Along with more traditional Swedish massages, shiatsu is offered at many spas and massage centers—or look it up under *massage* in your local Yellow Pages to find nearby practitioners.

Other types of touch therapy and bodywork range from *Rolfing*, a very deep and sometimes painful type of bodywork whose purpose is actually to restructure the body and bring it into better alignment, to the *Feldenkrais Technique*, which works mainly by improving posture through self-awareness of stance, gesture, and movement. If you're interested, many books are also available that explain the differences among the various bodywork and massage approaches.

REFLEXOLOGY

This is an ancient Chinese practice based on the principle that the feet reflect the state of every organ, muscle, and limb in the body. Working on the foot seems to relieve problems elsewhere in the body, providing a generalized sense of well-being. The theory is that when the foot is stimulated—pressed or massaged—in a certain area, the pressure stimulates nerve endings elsewhere. Energy flows through now unlocked passageways and flushes out "crystals," waste deposits that have blocked the energy from passing through the whole body. Although most qualified reflexologists don't claim to actually cure disease by manipulating the feet, advocates say that reflexology works incredibly well to release tension, stress, headaches, and backaches, among other urban ills.

Even if it were *only* a foot massage, it would work wonderfully for attitude. Think about it: If your feet don't hurt, don't you instantly walk taller? Call the International Institute of Reflexology at 813-343-4811 for a list of qualified practitioners in your area.

REIKI

Reiki, a system of healing what ails you by means of channeling energy from another person to you, is growing increasingly popular. This energy, called the universal life force energy, is drawn by the unwell person from the healthy healer. There's no rubbing involved, just passive touching, and although it sounds far-out, it's becoming almost mainstream—that's how many people swear by it. It's noninvasive, so it can't hurt, and it's enormously relaxing and rejuvenating. You can call the American International Reiki Association (813-347-3454) to locate Reiki practitioners in your area.

TRANSCENDENTAL MEDITATION (TM)

Transcendental Meditation, based on classic Hindu meditation techniques, is said to induce a state of restful alertness, increasingly popular these days. People say that the mantra they learn to repeat during their everyday activities (you can do it on a bus, at a lecture, at your job) gives them an unparalleled sense of serenity, self-confidence, and relaxation. For information call 888-LEARN-TM.

YOGA

If the city where you live seems calmer these days, the reason may be a new but ancient process of physical and mental training. Yoga is a mystical Hindu system of meditation, breathing, and physical activity that integrates the body and the mind—and it's said to be an incomparable attitude lifter. Unlike traditional strength training with weights and machines, which can strain muscles and ligaments, yoga makes the body more flexible, the mind more peaceful, and the spirit more, well, *spiritual*, while you remain virtually injury-free. Almost every gym offers yoga classes.

Similar in many ways to yoga is the increasingly popular *Pilates* strength-training approach, which emphasizes body posture and carriage: Learning to walk the power walk with shoulders and back held straight is a giant step toward developing *attitude*.

STRESS BUSTERS

Being bowed down by stress doesn't do a whole lot for attitude. Try these three simple stress busters:

HERBAL TREATMENTS

Certain herbs, used in the form of teas, capsules, and oils, are said to do wonders toward strengthening the nervous system so you're less vulnerable to stress. Try passion flower, chamomile, oatstraw, kava, and skullcap in tea or in capsule form. An aromatic bath sweetened with a few drops of a soothing essential oil (ylang ylang, vetiver, or sandalwood) relieves anxiety, insomnia, tension headaches, and tight muscles. You can find these and other herbs and oils in health food stores.

TIME MANAGEMENT

Block out priorities, which means deciding what activities you can throw out of your life to give yourself more *self* time. For example, don't answer every phone call or E-mail that comes in on your machines—are you a slave to others' needs? No, darling. And do you really want to see that awful movie and come away feeling like you've wasted a little bit more of life? Curl up with a great book instead.

SUPPLEMENT YOUR BODY

Okay, I'm a vitamin nut—and certain vitamins seem to be calming. Check with your own physician to see what she suggests, but Dr. Earl Mindell, the author of *Secret Remedies*, suggests 1,000 mg of methylsulfonylmethane (MSM) and 250 mg of magnesium daily; 25 to 50 mg of vitamin B complex two to three times daily; 500 mg of calcium at bedtime; and, if you can get it, sexual activity before sleep (everyone knows that's a stress buster!).

RITUAL

A simple ritual—like having a cup of tea at teatime—is veddy veddy, nice and does wonders for the attitude. Call the poshest hotel in your town and ask if they offer tea service. Dress up and go and have a spot of tea with a beloved friend.

The bottom line for developing a marvelous attitude: You need to be aware. You need to be unafraid of taking small risks. You need to feel good.

So be kind to yourself. Pay attention to the needs of a healthy body and an adventuresome spirit. Get into the habit of respecting your intuition as well as your conscious thoughts and opinions.

You've heard someone say disparagingly of another, "Well, will you look at her, she's got attitude." Don't knock attitude. It's what makes you stand out, makes you different. I'll tell you a secret. You've heard that blondes have more fun? Wrong, and I ought to know. It's women with *attitude* who have more fun.

SCENES FROM A CITY.

Finally, we could have picked New York or Washington, Chicago, Dallas, or Atlanta, sure—but strolling through the City of Angels and its environs on a hot Saturday, we found proof of that Big City Look attitude in just a few typical vignettes. Here it is—the look of one big city.

Los Angeles, California.

We found it in the attitude of two roller-skating partners—she with a scarf knotted around the hips of her leotard, he showing off his natural grace and pride.

We found it in two shoppers on Rodeo Drive wearing their shades, signature purses, high heels, cigarette pants, and fitted shirts—and an air of expectation . . . What great thing can I buy next?

We found it on Venice Beach in the grin and person of a pretty blond starlet—all fitness and flash, her navel showing above her cutoff jeans, her tanned body, her arm, wrist, and knee pads protecting her as she Rollerbladed her way to the studio.

We found it in the powerful muscle definition of a trainer to the stars practicing an early-morning warmup on deserted L.A. streets. Notice her pretty earrings; muscles or not, she won't leave home without them.

Finally, we found it in the sheer exuberance of two little girls doing cartwheels at sunset on Venice Beach—two little girls practicing for the Big City Look.

EPILOGUE

There it is.

I hope that reading this book has helped you deconstruct the way the woman with The Look styles her hair, makeup, clothes, and attitude. I hope you've also come to see that the place where you live helps determine the prettiest and most sophisticated way for you to look.

We can sum up the essence of this book quite simply with four words.

Classical: Wear the classics often. From top to bottom, let your clothes consist of fine fabrics and ageless style. Let your hair and makeup be elegant and simple as well.

Original: Add a touch of originality to those classics—a personal signature that says you. Something different. Something rare. Maybe even something funny.

Open-minded: Stretch yourself, take risks, open your heart to new ideas and new ways to exercise mind and body; develop attitude.

Location: The only thing to consider when buying real estate, say the experts, is location, location, location. When buying the Big City Look, it's the same: Your location, your own neck of the woods, your sense of place determine the most appropriate look for you.

So the next time you're walking on the main street in the city, town, or village where you live, watch out for her—that woman with the Big City Look. She may be short or tall, blond or brunette, young or old . . . it doesn't matter. You'll know her. You'd know her in the city, on the beach, on the moon. Anywhere. She holds her head high as she bops down the avenue, wearing the shades *and* the attitude. She's stunning, and she looks like she's fun—just the kind of woman you'd like to have for a role model or a best friend.

Or wait—is that a mirror you're passing? Is the woman with the Big City Look . . . you? Why not?

ACKNOWLEDGMENTS

Deep, deep thanks to Vincent's store—the fabulous Saks Fifth Avenue—which sustains the Big City Look in cities, big and small, all over the world. We're especially appreciative to the powers that be at Saks for generously allowing us the use of the most extraordinary fashions seen throughout this book. In particular, gratitude to . . .

* JACQUELINE LIVIDINI, vice president, public relations and special events—a consummate professional and someone who makes things happen, and thanks also to her skilled assistant, LORI RHODES. Deep appreciation also to PHILLIP MILLER, chairman and chief executive officer; LAWRENCE HILL, senior vice president and general manager, New York; BRIAN E. KENDRICK, vice chairman and chief operating officer; and JEANNE B. DANIEL, executive vice president, merchandising.

More thanks are due to . . .

* THE EXTRAORDINARY STARS OF THIS BOOK—the women who epitomize the Big City Look—and have allowed us to photograph them. A special thank you to our Ford cover model, Nina Bellanger.

* RICHARD SHEVLIN for saving our lives—that's all. What a friend! And thanks to Sybil for giving us Richard.

* ROSE MARIE BRAVO, former president of Saks Fifth Avenue and presently president of Burberry's International, for immediately understanding the concept of this book—and helping us fulfill it.

* DONNA MCPHERSON, Vincent's intrepid, beautiful, and creative assistant. Thanks also to the tireless DEBORAH WYNNS, JOEY LEE, and Vincent's makeup assistant, MELANIE SWANSON.

* THE FASHION INSTITUTE OF TECHNOLOGY, a wonderful big city school (New York City, to be exact) that understands the power of The Look—and teaches it in myriad ways to its students. In particular, at FIT, JACQUES HUTZLER of the department of photography and DOROTHY LOVERRO of the department of illustration, who have been such valuable resources for this book.

* Our soon-to-be-famous, absolutely extraordinary photographer, ALEX CAO, and our very talented illustrator, AKIKO OGURO, both products of FIT.

* The great ELIZABETH ARDEN RED DOOR SPAS AND SALONS, whose leadership advances the Big City Look, especially to DAVID STOUP, president and CEO, and ARTHUR FABRICANT, chairman of Elizabeth Arden Salons Inc.

* BARBARA DEMOULIN of the *Fashion Planet Internet Magazine*, a generous and warm resource. Also funny.

* World-renowned photographers HARRY BENSON of *Life* magazine for his wonderful photograph of Texan Liz Smith, PATRICK DEMARCHELIER for the extraordinary photo of Isabella Rossellini, DENIS REGGIE of Denis Reggie Photographers in Atlanta for the stellar photograph of Atlantan Sharon Sadler, JAMES RICHTER of the Gittings Portrait Studio in Fort Worth for the photographs of Texans Beth DeCluett and Rosie Montcrief and photographer RAY PAYNE for an additional photograph of Rosie Montcrief. We also thank SANTE D'ORAZIO for the superb photos of Julia Ormond and Vanessa Williams, HARRY LANGDON for the wonderful photo of Morgan Fairchild, NANCY ELLISON for the smashing photo of actress Anne Archer, and JILL LYNNE for the memorable photo of identically bobbed Liz and Hillary Rodham Clinton.

* The ESTÉE LAUDER COMPANIES for their generous and careful help in documenting the regionality of cosmetics and skin care—in particular, the most efficient woman in America—MARGARET STEWART. Special gratitude to CHERYL CRISPEN, vice president, marketing, Estée Lauder; KAREN O'CONNOR, vice president, administration, Estée Lauder; ANDREA SARKISIAN, executive director, Global Communications, Origins; EVA LESKO, executive director, Global Communications, Clinique USA; BETH MANN of Bobbi Brown Essentials; and the extraordinary, irrepressible EVELYN LAUDER herself. Evelyn, daily, invents the Big City Look.

* BRIAN LABORSKY, president and CEO of Premiere Salons, a colleague and early supporter of *Big City Look*.

* We are immensely grateful for the life of the late CONNIE CLAUSEN, cherished and sheltering agent and friend. Of course, we are thankful also for the marvelous (and stylish) STEDMAN MAYS and MARY TAHAN of the Clauson, Mays and Tahan Literary Agency and also for CHARLES BJORKLUND and his discerning eye.

* Vincent's special thanks to Drs. DANIEL BAKER, DEBRA JALIMAN, LUIS NAVARRO, and ROSALINDA RUBINSTEIN. They know why.

* Most of all, our gratitude to our brilliant editor, DIANE REVERAND, who *owns* the Big City Look. And to SOL SLOTNIK who appreciates The Look. Our own appreciation also *to* these talented people in Diane's department at Cliff Street Books—KRISTA STROEVER and DAVID FLORA—and to HarperCollins art director JOSEPH MONTEBELLO.

* And, finally, love and thanks to Sherry's crew—LARRY, JENNIFER, STEVEN, SUSAN, ADAM, BECKY, JOSH, and JULIA BULIA.